The Terror Enigma

The Terror Enigma

◆

9/11 and the Israeli Connection

Justin Raimondo

iUniverse, Inc.

New York Lincoln Shanghai

The Terror Enigma
9/11 and the Israeli Connection

iUniverse, Inc.

For information address:
iUniverse, Inc.
2021 Pine Lake Road, Suite 100
Lincoln, NE 68512
www.iuniverse.com

ISBN: 0-595-29682-3

Printed in the United States of America

Contents

Introduction

"Remember 9/11!" is the rallying cry of the War Party—but what we are remembering is a half-truth. This book draws the curtain on the largely ignored pre-history of 9/11, a disturbing series of events leading up to the worst terrorist attack in American history, and points a finger at a key collaborator—the intelligence services of the state of Israel.

We know that an underground terrorist network, loosely affiliated with Al Qaeda, developed the plans that culminated in the 9/11 attacks over a period of at least five years. During that time, the 9/11 conspirators infiltrated the U.S., where they trained as pilots, waiting for The Day. What most do not know, however, is that, starting at least as far back as January 2001, a parallel invasion of American shores was launched by Israeli agents masquerading as traveling "art students." It is fairly common knowledge that the leader of the hijackers, Mohammed Atta, and some of the others, based their operations in south Florida, and especially in and around the town of Hollywood, where Atta lived for a time with some of his fellow conspirators. The Israelis also based their operations in Hollywood, and kept a close, virtually silent watch on the terrorist ringleader and his friends.

The reaction of horror and revulsion to the worst terrorist attack in American history was, to all within sight of the World Trade Center, well nigh unanimous—but not quite. A few hours after the attacks, as the burning twin towers sent skyward a plume of smoke and flame that could be seen for miles, five Israeli men laughed and acted in a celebratory manner, photographing each other against the backdrop of the catastrophe. From their vantage point in Liberty State Park, overlooking the Hudson river, the men were afforded a sweeping view of the Manhattan skyline: according to witnesses, the sight of the catastrophe had them cheering. They later insisted that they were merely "documenting" the event, but their accuser—a woman who saw them from the window of her high-rise apartment—found their behavior so suspicious that she wrote down the license plate number of their van and called the police.

As America contemplates the conquest of the Middle East, and the last vestiges of constitutional government are swept away by a tsunami of war hysteria, the memory of what happened on that autumn day has been thoroughly mythologized. The official legend of 9/11 was succinctly summarized by the President of the United States in his address to a joint session of Congress shortly after the event:

> Americans have many questions tonight. Americans are asking: Who attacked our country? The evidence we have gathered all points to a collection of loosely affiliated terrorist organizations known as al Qaeda. They are the same murderers indicted for bombing American embassies in Tanzania and Kenya, and responsible for bombing the USS Cole.[1]

But that was hardly the question that most needed asking. Bin Laden and his associates were the prime suspects from the beginning, and no one was surprised when the terrorist leader effectively claimed responsibility. For the central enigma of 9/11, one that that President Bush failed to mention in his speech, is surely this: How did 19 hijackers manage to pull off the most spectacular terrorist act in modern history—in the face of so many warnings, and so many US tax dollars spent combating terrorism—without the assistance of any state?[2]

The sheer shock of 9/11 made it impossible to think clearly about what had happened, but the collective numbness wore off eight months later, when the Bush administration admitted to having been warned in advance. BUSH KNEW! screamed the *New York Post* headline, and conspiracy theorists had a field day.[3] But the irony was that, apparently alone among the world's leaders, Bush *didn't* know—and, we have to ask, why not?

Although administration officials at first denied that they had even a hint of what was to come, it now turns out that government agencies were literally awash with warnings from foreign intelligence services—including the British,[4] the French,[5] the Germans,[6] the Russians,[7] the Argentines,[8] the Israelis,[9] the Egyptians,[10] the Moroccans, and the Jordanians.[11]

The Israelis warned us, in August 2001, when they sent a delegation to Washington, handed over a list of nineteen individuals in the U.S. whom they believed to be planning terrorist activities, and issued a non-specific warning that a major terrorist attack was afoot. Yet there is every indication that the Mossad knew about Atta and his gang long before they let U.S. law enforcement in on the secret.

In the months prior to 9/11, the Mossad had launched a major covert operation in the U.S., involving hundreds of agents, who not only kept a close watch on the terrorists, but also effectively blinded U.S. anti-terrorism investigators to the activities of Al Qaeda on American shores. The evidence is in the U.S. gov-

ernment's own documents, leaked by its own employees, and in its public pro-
nouncements before the decision was made to quash this story at any cost.

In March 2001, the National Counterintelligence Center—whose mandate,
established in 1995, empowers it to identify and assess possible threats to U.S.
national security—posted the following warning on its website:

> In the past six weeks, employees in federal office buildings located throughout
> the United States have reported suspicious activities connected with individu-
> als representing themselves as foreign students selling or delivering artwork.
> Employees have observed both males and females attempting to bypass facility
> security and enter federal buildings. If challenged, the individuals state that
> they are delivering artwork from a studio in Miami, Florida, called Universal
> Art, Inc, or that they are art students and are looking for opinions regarding
> their work. These individuals have been described as aggressive. They attempt
> to engage employees in conversation rather than giving a sales pitch.[12]

At that point, two had been arrested and taken into custody for immigration
violations: the suspects were in possession of counterfeit immigration papers and
identification. Later, many more would be picked up—nearly 200, as far as anyone can tell[13]—and summarily deported back to their country of origin: Israel.
No one took much notice at the time, but if they had they would have stumbled
on yet another disturbing aspect to this story. The NCIC also warned that "these
individuals have also gone to the private residences of senior federal officials
under the guise of selling art." As to how they discovered the home addresses of
these senior officials, the NCIC did not say.

The NCIC alert was the earliest premonition, some six months before the
event, of 9/11. It was the first known instance—and possibly the last—in which
the "anti-terrorism" apparatus set up by the U.S. government actually worked, to
some extent. The NCIC ended its warning with, as it turned out, an accurate
assessment of the threat:

> Other reporting indicates that there may be two groups involved, and they
> refer to themselves as "Israeli art students." One group has an apparently legit-
> imate money-making goal while the second, perhaps a non-Israeli group, may
> have ties to a Middle Eastern Islamic fundamentalist group. Federal employees
> observing any activity similar to that described above should report their
> observations to appropriate security officials.[14]

And report they did. Indeed, so many accounts of Israeli "art student" sight-
ings poured in, from such a wide variety of federal agencies, that they were com-

piled in a secret government dossier. Their mode of operation was always the same: they would enter a U.S. federal facility, even some that were unmarked, and make their pitch about selling their "artwork," aggressively seeking entry through back doors and generally acting as if they were casing the joint. Since the nation's frontline fighters in the "war on drugs" had, for some reason, attracted the particular attention of these alleged "art students," this document, which only came to light after 9/11, seems to have been compiled and written up by the internal security unit of the Drug Enforcement Agency (DEA), in cooperation with the Immigration and Naturalization Service, sometime in the summer, 2001.[15]

The incidents were ongoing "since at least the beginning of 2000," and increased in November: after April 2001, "the number of reported incidents...declined, however, the geographic spread of the incidents" was extended "to Wisconsin, Oklahoma, and Los Angeles." In addition to DEA offices, these "art students" also descended on a number of other law enforcement and Department of Defense facilities spread across the continental United States. The majority of recorded incidents, however, seem to have occurred in the southern half of the country, with the epicenter of activity located in southern Florida. DEA investigators associated with the agency's Office of Security Programs apparently became convinced that, as the report put it:

> The nature of the individuals' conduct, combined with intelligence information and historical information regarding past incidents involving Israeli Organized Crime, leads us to believe the incidents may well be an organized intelligence gathering activity.[16]

These were no ordinary Israeli "tourists," as they claimed when confronted. While all Israelis must serve some time in the military, an unusually high proportion of these "students" were deployed in elite specialized units. The DEA report lists name, rank, and serial number: Itay Simon, Marina Glickman, Dilka Borenstein are all described as "former" members of Israeli military intelligence. Zeev Miller is identified as a "combat engineer," and Ofir Navron is a "bomb disposal expert." Aran Ofek, the son of a two-star Israeli general, was apprehended in Dallas. Taken together, their credentials are impressive: "intelligence officer," "electronic intercept operator," "special forces," "demolition/explosive ordnance expert." These young Israelis could be considered students of "art" only if we're talking about the art of war.[17]

In addition to the NCIC alert, there were a few, scattered local news reports on the "Israeli art student" phenomenon. KHOU television, in Houston, did a few stories, reporting on October 1, '01 that, earlier in the year, groups of Israelis were caught sneaking into "federal buildings and defense sites," and, in Dallas, "the so-called students hit early this year at the city's FBI building, the Drug Enforcement Administration and at the Earle Cabell Federal building, where guards found one student wandering the halls with a floor plan of the building."[18]

The suggestion of an Israeli connection to the events surrounding 9/11 did not spring, full blown, like Athena from the head of Zeus. It had been hovering in the background, implied in disparate news accounts such as the one about a group of Israelis picked by the FBI after they were spotted in Liberty State Park, Jersey City, NJ, laughing and giving each other high-fives as the World Trade Center burned on the other side of the river. An astonishing story in the Bergen, New Jersey *Record* [September 12, 2001], describes how five men—"Israeli tourists"—were picked up 8 hours after the WTC attack, "carrying maps linking them to the blasts." According to this news account by staff writer Paulo Lima:

> [S]ources close to the investigation said they found other evidence linking the men to the bombing plot. "There are maps of the city in the car with certain places highlighted," the source said. "It looked like they're hooked in with this. It looked like they knew what was going to happen when they were at Liberty State Park."[19]

Lima reports that the five "tourists" had been picked up by local police after receiving the following alert from the FBI:

> Vehicle possibly related to New York terrorist attack. White, 2000 Chevrolet van with New Jersey registration with "Urban Moving Systems" sign on back seen at Liberty State Park, Jersey City, NJ, at the time of first impact of jetliner into World Trade Center. Three individuals with van were seen celebrating after initial impact and subsequent explosion. FBI Newark Field Office requests that, if the van is located, hold for prints and detain individuals.[20]

Then there was the story about the two employees of the Odigo Company, an Israeli-based "instant-messaging" software firm, with New York offices in the vicinity of the WTC, who received computer messages in the hours before disaster struck that the World Trade Center would be hit. I was so skeptical of this report, published in *Ha'aretz*, an Israeli daily newspaper, that I wrote the author: he confirmed the contents of these mysterious missives and cited his sources.[21]

But these reports attracted little if any notice, and it wasn't until after 9/11 that this whole operation began to surface in major media.

On November 23, 2001, the *Washington Post* ran a news story detailing how, along with the 1,000 or so Muslim Middle Easterners jailed in the Ashcroft Sweep, 60 Israelis had been picked up and held, not just for routine visa violations, but in connection with the 9/11 investigation. The *Post*'s subhead read: "Government calls Several Cases 'of Special Interest,' Meaning Related to Post-Attacks Investigation."[22]

According to the story by John Mintz, INS officials in Cleveland and St. Louis testified in court that these Israelis were "of special interest to the government"—putting them in the same category as hundreds of mostly Arab men rounded up by the feds since the attacks.

A portion of the whale had surfaced. Over the next eight or nine months the rest of the story would come out, obscured by denials all around and submerged by a media oddly indifferent to a story with an obvious 9/11 angle. "It is rather strange," remarked *Jane's Defense Intelligence Digest*, "that the US media seems to be ignoring what may well be the most explosive story since the 11 September attacks—the alleged break-up of a major Israeli espionage operation in the USA."[23]

Another obscuring cloud was rampant Judeo-phobia in the Muslim world. In the days and weeks after the twin towers went down, perfervid rumors of Israeli responsibility for the attack roiled some sectors of the Arab media, with the former Imam of New York City's biggest mosque refusing to rule it out. The pro-Israel pundits had a field day with this, pointing to these comments as proof positive that the Arab mind was fundamentally and perhaps irreversibly deformed by "Islamo-fascism" and hatred. But given the irrefutable fact that 60 Israeli citizens were rounded up and held—under conditions of great secrecy—in connection with the 9/11 investigation, it was no longer tenable to dismiss the possibility of an Israeli angle in this story.

Although the *Post* blandly assured readers that the Israeli detainees were "observing a time-honored tradition in their country, touring the world after their mandatory service in the Israeli military," we were also informed that "a number of them had served in counterterrorist units in Israel."

Clearly, these were no ordinary Israeli tourists—and spying is, indeed, a time-honored tradition.

An eerie pattern began to emerge early on, and, as it happened, I was in a position to see it take shape out of the post-9/11 blizzard of news stories and speculation. As the editorial director of Antiwar.com, a news and commentary site dedicated to opposing U.S. intervention around the world, I was immersed in megabytes of data from the moment the World Trade Center was struck by the first plane, and have remained so to this day. After 9/11, we are often reminded, "everything changed"—and that was certainly true for Antiwar.com, which saw its audience skyrocket. In the space of a single day, Antiwar.com went from being an outlet for material of interest to a rather specialized group of people to a site of vital interest to a broad and diverse audience. We went from being focused on news of far-away conflicts that few knew or cared about to news about the new world that was taking shape before our eyes, George W. Bush's post-9/11 world of perpetual war for perpetual "peace."

In the aftermath of the terrorist atrocities, the War Party reared up like a demon out of Hell, roaring its eagerness to get on with the fight and put the entire Arab world to the sword. The bodies had yet to be recovered from the ruins before the neoconservative faction of the Republican party began to agitate for a civilizational war against Islam, and the President of the United States, in declaring a "war on terrorism," echoed their Manichean mantra: "You're either with us," declared George W. Bush, "or you're with the terrorists."

It was all very simple and convenient for supporters of Israel, who figured prominently among the Washington warhawks. Whatever ambivalence Washington policymakers had about their "special relationship" with Israel was dropped, and U.S. policy tilted toward Tel Aviv even more than before. The cries for war with Iraq, which had been present as low-level background noise, grew louder the day after 9/11, and were echoed by the White House. "We are all Israelis now," wrote Martin Peretz, in *The New Republic*, a slogan that succinctly summarized the neoconservative foreign policy prescription for the post-9/11 world.[24]

But we *aren't* all Israelis now, I thought, as I read the *Washington Post*'s account of the Israeli detainees. If Israel's enemies are now *our* enemies, then why was the U.S. government holding dozens of Israelis incommunicado, under the same legal rationale as Arabs being held in the terrorism investigation? The Israelis had been picked up because they were of "special interest" to the U.S. government, just like their Semitic brothers of the Muslim persuasion. I was struck by this legal equivalence, which implied the sort of "moral equivalence" Israel's apologists usually found intolerable.

Yet hardly a word of public protest was uttered at their incarceration, and, furthermore, nothing more was heard of these mysterious Israelis languishing in American prisons for unknown reasons. The nation was still reeling from the shock, and outrage, that accompanied 9/11 to notice this seemingly minor anomaly.

No one, that is, but a relatively obscure columnist for a non-"mainstream" website. But Antiwar.com, even with its greatly increased audience, didn't amount to anything but a faint blip on the screen, and it looked like we were alone in emphasizing the importance of this story. Antiwar.com had neither the resources to launch a proper investigation nor anything near the influence wielded by the major media. If there was an Israeli connection to 9/11, then it would have to be left to the "mainstream" media to uncover it. It was a depressing thought.

In the immediate post-9/11 atmosphere, when it seemed to many perfectly reasonable to proclaim "we are all Israelis now," raising the possibility of an Israeli role in 9/11 seemed completely out of the question as far as the major media were concerned. That, at least, was my own gloomy assessment, but, as it turned out, I couldn't have been more wrong. This story was too big, its implications too suggestive, to stay penned up in a relatively obscure corner of cyberspace.

The breakthrough came on December 11, 2001, in a big way, and from an unexpected source. Fox News, the right-wing voice of the Bush administration and the most openly pro-Israel of all the American television networks, ran the first in a series of investigative reports that blew the whistle on a multi-tentacled Israeli spy network operating on American soil—and openly posed the question of whether the Israelis had foreknowledge of 9/11.

1

The Israeli Connection

What is striking about Fox News reporter Carl Cameron's portrait of Israel's spy network in the U.S. is the sheer vastness of his subject. The broad scope of the operation, with its many fronts and activities conducted from coast to coast, had all the aspects of a major military campaign. In the months leading up to 9/11, Cameron claimed, Israel was waging a covert war against its principal ally and benefactor, the United States. This was the clear import of Fox News anchorman Brit Hume's brief precis to Cameron's report:

> It has been more than 16 years since a civilian working for the Navy was charged with passing secrets to Israel. Jonathan Pollard pled guilty to conspiracy to commit espionage and is serving a life sentence. At first, Israeli leaders claimed Pollard was part of a rogue operation, but later took responsibility for his work. Now Fox News has learned some U.S. investigators believe that there are Israelis again very much engaged in spying in and on the U.S., who may have known things they didn't tell us before September 11. Fox News correspondent Carl Cameron has details....[25]

Over four nights, Cameron reported the myriad details of Israel's far-flung underground army in the U.S. He noted the anomaly that no one else in the news media had thought significant enough to report, except for a perfunctory news item in the *Washington Post*: in the wake of September 11, more than 60 Israelis had been arrested in what appeared to be a major sweep. According to Cameron, among the detainees were active Israeli military officers. Some had failed polygraph tests when they were asked about "surveillance activities against and in the United States."[26]

Cameron showed how the Mossad had thoroughly penetrated top secret communications systems. He cited veteran law enforcement agents afraid for their jobs if they so much as questioned Israel's role. But what really caught the attention of viewers was the following statement from his first broadcast:

> There is no indication that the Israelis were involved in the 9-11 attacks, *but investigators suspect that they Israelis may have gathered intelligence about the attacks in advance, and not shared it.* A highly placed investigator said there are—quote—'tie-ins.' But when asked for details, he flatly refused to describe them, saying—quote—"evidence linking these Israelis to 9-11 is classified. I cannot tell you about evidence that has been gathered. It's classified information."[27]

If the Israelis knew, and didn't warn us—then the conventional black-and-white version of what happened that day is subverted by shades of ambiguity. If Cameron is right, then Israel, along with Al Qaeda, shares moral culpability for 9/11.

Cameron's bombshell should have provoked a frenzy of media interest and calls for an official investigation. That no such call was ever heard is a testament to the special immunity that Israel has enjoyed, in the eyes of both the media and U.S. government, and is a story in itself.

Any negative story involving Israel poses a dilemma for reporters. Another consequence of 9/11 has been a concerted campaign by American supporters of Israel to shape the news to their liking. Boycotts, email campaigns, a relentless barrage of baseless accusations—these weapons are by now familiar to all journalists, who have seen them wielded time and again against their colleagues. No one wants to risk their career without good reason, and journalists are no exception to the rule. Yet Cameron did not hesitate to state his startling thesis plainly, from the outset, in terms that should have sent shockwaves through the media and the political world.

Cameron's willingness to stir up a hornets' nest stemmed from the solidity and integrity of his sources in law enforcement. These were, after all, frontline fighters in the "war on terrorism," and they had come to him with a story no reporter worth his salt could refuse. They had come to him saying that Israel's underground army in the U.S. had both the means and the opportunity to know what al-Qaeda was up to—so why didn't they tell us?

In the first part of his report, Cameron lays out his thesis of Israeli foreknowledge of 9/11, and in subsequent parts shows they had the means and the opportunity to acquire this knowledge. Episode one focuses on a single aspect of what was a many-layered Israeli intelligence operation, one that became increasingly visible in the months preceding 9/11—so visible that it became the subject of a government investigation:

Numerous classified documents obtained by Fox News indicate that even prior to September 11, as many as 140 other Israelis had been detained or arrested in a secretive and sprawling investigation into suspected espionage by Israelis in the United States. Investigators from numerous government agencies are part of a working group that's been compiling evidence since the mid-90s. These documents detail hundreds of incidents in cities and towns across the country that investigators say—quote—"may well be an organized intelligence gathering activity."[28]

What we know of these documents is that they included a 60-page report compiled by a number of federal agencies detailing the activities of people who claimed to be Israeli "art students," and whose determination to gain access to U.S. government facilities—including military bases and other defense-related buildings—provoked a security alert at the national level.[29]

In the gray, matter-of-fact bureaucratese so typical of a government document, the "Israeli Art Student Papers"—leaked some months later—confirmed Cameron's contention that an underground apparatus of Israeli agents, centered in Florida and Texas but extending nationwide, carried out extensive operations in the months prior to 9/11. Their targets included the Drug Enforcement Administration, the Immigration and Naturalization Service, the Federal Protective Service, the Bureau of Alchohol, Tobacco, and Firearms, the Federal Bureau of Investigation, a host of state and federal courthouses and other buildings, as well as military bases.

The leaked document describes in excruciating detail the doggedly persistent efforts of Israelis claiming to be "art students" to get into the offices and even the homes of federal law enforcement agents and government officials.

From the report we get a broad overview of the activities of Israel's clandestine army, if not its strategic objectives or motives. These covert actions had commenced "since at least the beginning of 2000," right up until the weeks before 9/11. The geographical reach of the operation was nationwide: although concentrated in the southwest and Florida, it stretched over at least 40 states. According to the report: "The Hollywood, Florida, area seems to be a central point for these individuals, with several having addresses in this area."

A March 5 [2002] article in *LeMonde* by Sylvain Cypel was more specific: "More than a third of these 'students' claimed residence in Florida," and "at least five were intercepted in Hollywood, and two in Fort Lauderdale." Cypel points out the proximity of the two cities, and reminds us that "at least 10 of the 19 terrorists of 9/11 were residing in Florida." Furthermore, Hollywood, a town of some 25,000 souls, north of Miami, was a major nexus of Israel's spy network *and* the Muslim terrorist cell responsible for 9/11, as Cameron noted and Cypel concurred:

> Four of the five members of the group that diverted American Airlines flight number 11—Mohammed Atta, Abdulaziz Al-Omari, Walid and Waïl Al-Shehri, as well as one of the five terrorists of United flight 175, Marwan Al-Shehhi—resided all at various times in…Hollywood, Florida. As for Ahmed Fayez, Ahmed and Hamza Al-Ghamdi and Mohand Al-Shehri, who took over United flight 75, like Saïd Al-Ghamdi, Ahmed Al-Haznawi and Ahmed Al-Nami, of United flight 93 which crashed September 11 in Pennsylvania, and Nawaq Al-Hamzi, of AA flight 77 (crashed into the Pentagon), they all at one time resided at Delray Beach, in the north of Fort Lauderdale.[30]

The Israelis were clearly engaged in a large-scale intelligence-gathering operation designed to keep a watch on Islamist terrorist cells. This conclusion is buttressed by the second part of Cameron's blockbuster report that showed the Israelis certainly had the means to keep track of the hijackers—and of American law enforcement, too. According to Cameron:

> Fox News has learned that some American terrorist investigators fear certain suspects in the Sept. 11 attacks may have managed to stay ahead of them, by knowing who and when investigators are calling on the telephone.[31]

We are taken through an explanation of how and why virtually all telephone calls in the U.S. are billed by a single company, Amdocs Ltd., which just happens to be headquartered in Israel. Chances are that when you make a call, the record of the call and the billing is done through Amdocs. With a virtual monopoly in the U.S., and tentacles worldwide, this Israeli government-subsidized company is in a position to reap a considerable intelligence harvest. Cameron reports that "it is virtually impossible to make a call on normal phones without generating an Amdocs record of it." Amdocs denies any wrongdoing, but Cameron reports that, in 1999,

> The super secret National Security Agency, headquartered in northern Maryland, issued what's called a 'top secret sensitive compartmentalized information report,' TS/SCI, warning that records of calls in the United States were getting into foreign hands—in Israel, in particular.[32]

It's not that anyone is listening in on conversations, but that these methods are a way to know who is calling whom, when, and for how long—vital information in and of itself. Cameron assures us that the White House and the Pentagon are immune from such surveillance, but an article in *Insight*, the magazine put out by the *Washington Times*, showed how Israeli intelligence had thoroughly penetrated the communications system at the Clinton White House. According to co-authors J. Michael Waller and Paul M. Rodriguez, the FBI was

> Probing an explosive foreign-espionage operation that could dwarf the other spy scandals plaguing the U.S. government. *Insight* has learned that FBI counterintelligence is tracking a daring operation to spy on high-level U.S.officials by hacking into supposedly secure telephone networks. The espionage was facilitated, federal officials say, by lax telephone-security procedures at the White House, State Department and other high-level government offices and by a Justice Department unwillingness to seek an indictment against a suspect.[33]

"The espionage operation may have serious ramifications," wrote Waller and Rodriguez, "because the FBI has identified Israel as the culprit."

Dozens of officials confirmed the story, telling the authors of this fascinating piece how the Israelis had managed to penetrate not only State Department telephone lines, but also those in the White House, the Defense Department, and the Justice Department. That the President knew this at the time is beyond doubt; it came out, you'll remember, during l'affaire Lewinsky, when Monica testified that, on March 29, 1997, she and Clinton were desecrating the Oval Office and she specifically remembered it because, as the Starr Report put it:

> He suspected that a foreign embassy was tapping his telephones, and he proposed cover stories. If ever questioned, she should say that the two of them were just friends. If anyone ever asked about their phone sex, she should say that they knew their calls were being monitored all along, and the phone sex was just a put on.[34]

That "foreign embassy" was the Israelis'. It is eerie, in retrospect, to read the comments of the American intelligence and law enforcement officials who sourced this pioneering *Insight* piece. "It's a huge security nightmare," said one senior U.S. official. "The implications are severe," another unnamed official chimed in. "We're not even sure we know the extent of it," said a third high-ranking intelligence official. "All I can tell you is that we think we know how it was done. That alone is serious enough, but it's the unknown that has such deep consequences."[35]

As the Fox News revelations make all too clear, these consequences are a lot deeper than anyone, including Waller and Rodriguez, writing two years before 9/11, could possibly have imagined. Not even the treachery of Jonathan Pollard quite measures up to the scale and import of the spy operation uncovered by Cameron.

Pollard did enormous damage to U.S. intelligence operations around the world. Yet Cameron presents us with a picture of a covert action operating on a whole other level of complexity. Pollard's target was clearly the U.S. government: his purpose was to steal secrets, and, in the process, do enormous damage to U.S. intelligence assets worldwide. Operation Israeli "art student," however, took up more varied tasks. First, keeping an eye on the 4-8 million-strong American Muslim community, nearly 80 percent immigrants. Their purpose: to monitor radical Islamic organizations in the U.S. It is inconceivable, in retrospect, that the Israelis *didn't* conduct extensive surveillance in the U.S. prior to 9/11, directed at both the Americans *and* Islamist cells.

The third part of Cameron's series shows how the Israelis had access not only to phone records, but also to the wiretaps being conducted by U.S. law enforcement agencies. This access could have easily been provided, Cameron points out, by yet another hi-tech Israeli communications company, Comverse/Infosys, which operates as practically a branch of the Israeli government, and enjoys near monopolistic status here in the U.S.

When a call is made, it goes through a complicated network of routers and switchers. The way wiretapping works is that customized computers are linked to that network via specialized software, and the system intercepts, records, and stores wiretapped calls. But this system has a "back door" that could have easily been opened by Israeli intelligence. Comverse maintains a link to the wiretapping computers, on the grounds that it is necessary for system "maintenance." Over the opposition of some in law enforcement, this process was authorized by the 1994 Communications Assistance for Law Enforcement Act (CALEA). But that wasn't the end of it. According to Cameron:

> Attorney General John Ashcroft and FBI Director Robert Mueller were both warned Oct. 18 [2001] in a hand-delivered letter from fifteen local, state and federal law enforcement officials, who complained that 'law enforcement's current electronic surveillance capabilities are less effective today than they were at the time CALEA was enacted.[36]

But Ashcroft was too busy rounding up Arabs and closing down their organizations to worry about the wholesale penetration of American communications systems—including "secure" networks at the White House, the Defense Department, and law enforcement agencies—by the Israelis. Cameron cites several unnamed agents concerned about the ominous implications of the Israeli penetration, who say that even raising the issue is "career suicide."[37]

The idea that U.S. communications are so thoroughly compromised, as fantastic as it sounds, is all too believable given the advance of technology and the reputation of the Mossad. Truly shocking, however, is the story of just how this penetration came to be uncovered in the first place. As Cameron informs us: "On a number of cases, suspects that [U.S. law enforcement] had sought to wiretap and survey immediately changed their telecommunications processes. They started acting much differently as soon as those supposedly secret wiretaps went into place."[38]

In 1997, U.S. authorities were ready to swoop down on a major Los Angeles drug gang. The target was an organized crime syndicate headquartered in Israel, with branches in New York, Miami, Las Vegas, Canada, and Egypt. Their specialty: cocaine, ecstasy, and "sophisticated white-collar credit card and computer fraud."[39] But there was a problem: the feds' plan had gone awry, the bad guys remained elusive, and no one could figure out why. At least, not until the feds discovered that the Israeli Mafia had bugged their communications, and had each and every one of them under surveillance—even their home phones. They knew where agents lived, when and where they would be picking their children up from school, their whole routine. In what is perhaps a bit of an understatement, classified documents uncovered by Fox News aver that

> This compromised law enforcement communications between LAPD detectives and other assigned law enforcement officers working various aspects of the case. The organization discovered communications between organized crime intelligence division detectives, the FBI and the Secret Service.[40]

Law enforcement officials went into a state of panic, and immediately turned to what many had considered the potential source of a major security breach to begin with: our old friend Amdocs. While the company protests its innocence, Cameron echoes many in law enforcement who think Amdocs' secrets somehow got into the "wrong hands."

As to just how such technology passed from the Mossad into the hands of the Israeli Mafia—or vice-versa—is a question that has come up in the course of this inquiry, and may never be fully answered. But the interaction of these two elements—an alliance of a foreign intelligence agency with criminal elements in

America—is altogether plausible. The DEA report alluded to "historical information regarding past incidents involving Israeli Organized Crime."[41] After all, the
U.S. cooperated with the American Mafia in going after Castro, so why shouldn't
the Israelis recruit their own gangsters to do *their* dirty work?[42]

The addition of a criminal element to the mix of spies and terrorists intro-
duces a random factor—and a dangerous, potentially catalytic element—in the
sense that the actions of the others are fairly predictable. The behavior of those
Israeli "art students," for example, was entirely consistent with that of covert
agents tasked with casing U.S. government premises and identifying government
employees. The behavior of the nineteen Al Qaeda cadre tasked with blowing up
the World Trade Center and the Pentagon was even more predictable: to inflict
maximum damage at minimum cost.

But a criminal is ruled by his or her subjective desires and impulses, which
vary from individual to individual and cannot be predicted. Criminals are often
motivated by economic gain, but not always: power, "turf," vengeance, sadism
and sheer perversity enter the picture, too. Which is why any intelligence outfit
that links up with a crime syndicate is bound to suffer some "blowback," the
CIA's term for unintended consequences.[43]

The possible consequences of putting this sort of "wild card" into play may
well have been illustrated by a September 13 *New York Times* column by William
Safire, entitled "Inside the Bunker." According to Safire, he had a conversation
with an unnamed "high White House official," who told him that on 9/11 "a
threatening message received by the Secret Service was relayed to the agents with
the president that 'Air Force One is next.' According to the high official, American code words were used showing a knowledge of procedures that made the
threat credible."[44]

Safire claims this information was confirmed by Karl Rove, who told him the
President was about to return to Washington when the Secret Service "informed
him that the threat contained language that was evidence that the terrorists had
knowledge of his procedures and whereabouts."[45]

If the Bin Ladenites knew *that* much—in the same way those West Coast
Israeli gangsters knew every move the feds were going to make before they made
it—then *how* did they know it? There are only two possibilities:

1. Bin Laden's group has infiltrated the top echelons of the U.S.government,
    and knows its most intimate secrets, or

2. The information was passed to them through some third party with the
    means and the motive to acquire it.

Cameron's report, while fragmentary, provides the basis for understanding the context in which the events of 9/11 occurred. The Israeli "art students," the penetration of U.S.communications systems by Israeli agents and Israeli organized crime, the 200 Israeli detainees rounded up prior to and after 9/11: it all adds up to a covert Israeli operation conducted on a major scale. One that played a key role in the events leading up to 9/11 which is, in large part, indeterminate—but almost certainly not benevolent.

What we do know is this: in the months leading up to 9/11, hundreds of Israeli "art students" launched a nationwide covert operation aimed at U.S. government facilities, and set off alarms throughout the system. At the same time, the nineteen hijackers were training, reconnoitering, and preparing for The Day, ensconced at several abodes but mainly in southern Florida, the geographical locus of the Israeli spy operation.

What seems almost certain is that the Mossad has been keeping on eye on Islamists in America for years. Eager to protect their intelligence-gathering sources and methods, they could not reveal everything they knew without betraying the nature and extent of their American assets. If they were indeed watching the Ladenites, then this implies some degree of foreknowledge of the events surrounding 9/11, if not the precise nature, location, and timing of the operation itself.

The issue of who is to blame for those attacks is settled: clearly, Bin Laden and his associates are responsible. But if it turns out that it wasn't just the top leadership of Al Qaeda who had September 11 marked on their calendars, then it is useful to remember that there are degrees of blame, and that it must be apportioned out accordingly. Did a rogue element of Israeli intelligence have advance notice of the 9/11 terrorist attacks? Given the extent of the spy nest uncovered by Cameron, in that dark inaugural winter of the post-9/11 era, this was not an unreasonable question—and became even less so, in the months to come, as information was leaked by insiders, or discovered by happenstance.

That only a few in the "mainstream" media, aside from Cameron, cared to ask such a question delayed but did not derail the discovery process. Despite clouds of obfuscation issued with squid-like regularity by Israel's American lobby, periodic denials by U.S. and Israeli government officials, and smear campaigns conducted against anyone who so much as mentioned this story, it didn't die. Instead, it percolated underground, slowly but surely gathering momentum.

2

Delayed Reaction

To most of us, 9/11 was a bolt out of the blue, with no prelude and no precedent. But the view from inside the U.S. government must have looked far more threatening—and baffling. Because the threat seemed to be coming, prior to 9/11, not from Bin Laden, but—incredibly—from the Israelis, who, not content with having gained access to sensitive communications, were physically penetrating American military and government targets. Law enforcement authorities were in the midst of a massive crackdown on the Israeli incursion, when suddenly they were hit—from the other direction. The invasion of the Israeli "art students," the biggest spy operation in the U.S. since the days of the Cold War, provides the essential context for understanding the mystery of 9/11.

We are being kept in the dark about so many things, these days, in the name of "national security." But if Americans are going to be asked to give up our liberties, our peace of mind, and in some cases even our lives in an apparently eternal "war on terrorism," then we at least have a right to know who our enemies are. We know Bin Laden is responsible for the murder of 3000 people—but we still don't know how the terrorists managed to pull off such a well-organized and spectacular display of murderous skill, undetected—and unassisted by any state sponsor.

Much has been said—and nothing proved—about the alleged role of Iraq in all this. But, as Cameron's investigations showed, it was the Israelis, not the Iraqis, who were running a major covert operation in the U.S. at the time.

The Arab detainees have been the subjects of a national controversy between civil libertarians and the Bush administration. Attorney General John Ashcroft denounced those who would "scare peace-loving people with phantoms of lost liberty" as "aiding the terrorists,"[46] while on the other hand Arab-Americans and the ACLU rallied opposition to the round-up. But when it came to the Israeli detainees, there was no controversy, and virtually no mention of it in the national media with the exception of a piece by Gershom Gorenberg, in the *Washington*

Post, bemoaning the fate of Omer Gavriel Marmari, one of the five Israelis arrested in New Jersey hours after the World Trade Center attacks.[47]

Gorenberg didn't mention why Marmari and the others were arrested, that they had been picked up because they were acting suspiciously in the wake of the World Trade Center attacks, or that they were laughing uproariously at the sight of the twin towers aflame. Instead, we are told that the five were simply "arrested as suspected terrorists" without any further explanation. Marmari spent 45 days in solitary confinement, and, according to the testimony of his mother, was subjected to the further indignity of being addressed as "Omar" instead of Omer. When the FBI called her, in Israel, to question her about her son, the agent "pronounced his name as the Arabic 'Omar,' and repeatedly asked her to spell it. Her explanations that 'Omer' is a Hebrew name—and her reminders that her son is blond and blue-eyed—apparently didn't register. At 6 the next morning, another FBI agent was on the phone, asking the same questions."[48]

Not even blonde hair and blue eyes could get Mr. Marmari out of the trouble he was in. They put him in leg-irons, and he "was sometimes punished when he sang in his cell in an effort to stay sane. For a month, the five were interrogated as suspected terrorists." Again avoiding any mention of the circumstances surrounding their arrest and subsequent detention, Gorenberg informs us that Marmari and his four companions "were questioned about supposed connections to Israeli intelligence." As to what these young men have to say for themselves, they "won't talk to the press" because "they can't bear to relive their experiences."[49]

According to Gorenberg, it was all a mistake growing out of the FBI's incompetence:

> The people who investigated Omer Marmari and his four friends are responsible for tracking down Islamic extremists who attacked America. They are supposed to protect the country from future attacks. Apparently, they are so ignorant of the Middle East that they do not know the difference between Hebrew and Arabic. They did not grasp that young men who tried to fast on Yom Kippur, the Jewish Day of Atonement, were probably not Muslim fanatics. Even when provided information on the detainees from Israeli authorities—allies of America with considerable experience in fighting Islamic terror—the investigators didn't grasp that they were wasting their time on the wrong men. Frankly, I think this should keep John Ashcroft from sleeping at night.[50]

The arrest of suspected Mossad agents in connection with the 9/11 attacks must have kept a few Israeli government officials up all night as well—and with good reason.

Aside from Gorenberg's lone voice of protest, Jewish groups were not rallying to the defense of these poor defenseless Israelis, held without bail and without lawyers, for the most part, in very uncomfortable and worrisome circumstances. Doesn't anybody find this odd?

Even stranger was the similarly subdued response to the Fox News exposé. Mark Regev, a spokesman at the Israeli embassy in Washington, was quoted by the *Jerusalem Post* as saying: "The report on Fox News contains no quoted source, it has in no way demonstrated anything more than anonymous innuendo, and should be regarded accordingly. Israel does not spy on the United States of America."[51]

Does the name "Jonathan Pollard" ring a bell?

The law enforcement sources who utilized Cameron's voice to project their concerns didn't dare allow their names to be used: as Cameron related in his report, anyone who raises the question of Israeli spying in the U.S. is committing "career suicide."

The same fear permeated the Fourth Estate. Cameron and Fox News did not merely lay bare Israel's "sprawling" spy operation in the U.S., but also reported Israel's passive complicity with the perpetrators of the worst terrorist attack in American history. One would think that the sheer enormity of such a charge would provoke a storm of outrage from Israel's many defenders in the media: the columnists, the think-tankers, the publicists who dote on Ariel Sharon's every word.

The idea that there was not much of a defense because Cameron's claims could not be taken seriously belies the extreme sensitivity of the Jewish community and others to perceived anti-Jewish sentiment, either real or imagined. In the past, much less has been seized on as "evidence" of anti-Israel or anti-Jewish "bias" in the media. But not this time, when protests occurred almost exclusively behind the scenes. Instead of a public outcry, there was an ominous, one might almost say a *guilty* silence.

Months went by, and no one would touch this story. Perhaps the shock of 9/11 was still too fresh to allow for clear thought: indeed, for the next six months the country seemed positively groggy, like a fighter in the eighth round who's reeling on his feet. It was a grim holiday season, and a joyless January, but in February of the new year people began to wake from their self-imposed stupor and ask questions. While the attorney general was taking off after John Walker Lindh, what about the nearly criminal negligence of U.S. law enforcement agencies, who clearly experienced some kind of massive intelligence meltdown? Howard Kurtz expressed the bottled-up sentiments of many when he pointed out in the *Washington Post*:

> For five long months, almost no one has wanted to gripe about it out loud. The shock had not yet worn off. It was a matter for another time, another place. First we had to bury the dead, heal the wounded, hail the rescuers, win the war. But yesterday the subject resounded across the marble halls of Congress: How could we not have known?[52]

We'll never know the answer to that very pertinent question if CIA director George Tenet has his way. Tenet declined to discuss any "details" on the opening day of the Senate Intelligence Committee's "what went wrong" on 9/11 hearings, where he mostly got a free pass—except for this question from Senator Richard Shelby (R-Alabama): "Why were we utterly unaware of the planning and execution of the Sept. 11 attacks? In other words, what went wrong?"[53]

"Whatever went wrong, Mr. Tenet said, it was not because of laziness or lack of attention within the CIA," reported the *New York Times*. "'Intelligence will never give you 100 percent predictive capability.'"[54]

Furthermore, the *Times* reports, "The director objected to the very word 'failure' in connection with the intelligence-gathering ahead of the devastating surprise attacks on the World Trade Center and the Pentagon. 'Failure means no focus, no attention, no discipline,' Mr. Tenet said, waving his finger for emphasis."[55]

Tenet's definition of failure—not the inability to intercept threats, but the failure to focus on them in the first place—sets the bar of success low enough to discount the death of three thousand people. Is he saying that they *were* paying attention, and that they somehow—inexplicably—failed to do anything about it? As Kurtz points out, Tenet skirted all questions, and, instead, "warned of more terrorist attacks, always a natural headline-grabber." News reports of the hearings confirmed the efficacy of this strategy: most echoed his ominously vague warning about the continuing threat of a terrorist attack on U.S. territory. But Kurtz wants to know "how can we prevent future attacks if we don't understand how we missed the last one?"[56]

Americans outside the Washington beltway would tend to agree with Kurtz, but the politicians don't see it that way. CNN reported that the President personally called Senate Majority Leader Tom Daschle and asked him to limit the scope and depth of the congressional investigation into 9/11, and that Vice President

Cheney made the same request.[57] At the hearings Tenet was treated with great "deference," according to the *Times*, and Kurtz concurs: "Carefully, gingerly, without Enron-like sensationalism, lawmakers are trying to scrutinize this century's Pearl Harbor."[58]

Why such caution? The fear was that the investigation would be "too broad," and would prove to be a "distraction" away from the war on terrorism. Instead of delving into the crucial events that set the stage for 9/11, the focus of the hearings was on "systemic" problems within the intelligence community. But why would a broad approach necessarily "distract" us—unless the assumption is that it would uncover some shocking revelations?

This strange lack of investigative enthusiasm was not limited to lawmakers, but included Kurtz's fellow American journalists, who showed remarkably little interest in pursuing the biggest story of the past few decades. As Carl Cameron lamented in a CSPAN interview:

> The biggest story of our time, of Israel spying on all branches of the government, on all our intelligence agencies—in the CIA [Central Intelligence Agency], the DEA and the White House itself, is not picked up by the leading newspapers like the *New York Times* and the *Washington Post*.[59]

The *Post*, at least, would eventually be forced to pick up the story, if only to serve as a publicist for official government denials. In the meantime, for months there was nothing in the "mainstream" media, until, finally, the story was picked up overseas by *Le Monde*,[60] which based its story on a report published in the *Intelligence Online* newsletter. The *Intelligence Online* outfit, in possession of the secret report on those Israeli "art students," named names:

> A few of the operatives are well known in the Israeli intelligence community. The report cited the names of Peer Segalovitz (military registration number 5087989) and Aran Ofek, son of a renowned two-star general in the Israeli army. The network targeted some of the most sensitive sites in the U.S., such as Tanker Air Force Base near Oklahoma City. Indeed, the U.S. Air Force's Office of Special Investigation sent a letter to the Justice Department on May 16 of last year to ask for assistance in a case against four Israelis suspected of spying: Yaron Ohana, Ronen Kalfon, Zeev Cohen and Naor Topaz.[61]

Israel's underground army in the U.S. consisted of "around 20 units composed of between four and eight members each." More names are named:

Michael Calmanovic headed up the team in Irving, Texas, while Florida was the domain of Hanan Serfaty. Legum Yochai had charge of the Miami operation.[62]

The Fox News series is cited, by *Intelligence Online* and *Le Monde*, and the former provides a convenient online map of the Texas chapter of the "art students" underground apparatus, complete with names, arrival dates, corporate connections, when and where they were arrested, and their specific functions in the Israeli military-intelligence apparatus.[63] *Intelligence Online* also notes the Amdocs connection: these "art students" "cultivated contacts with Israeli information technology companies based in the U.S. and serving as regular suppliers to various U.S. federal agencies, such as Amdocs" and others.

Le Monde provides a telling detail: six of the apprehended Israelis carried cell phones bought and paid for by a former Israeli vice consul to the United States. In addition, two of these "students" were high-flying world-travelers of a peculiar sort: in a single day, they had traveled from Hamburg to Miami to visit an FBI agent in his home, boarded a flight to Chicago to drop in at the home of a Justice Department agent, and then jumped on a flight to Toronto.[64]

As the embargo on the Israeli spy story began to break down, with reports from the British media filtering into the U.S. and Canada, the *Washington Post*—the original source of the news that 60 Israelis had been detained—ran what is fated to become the standard denial: "'This seems to be an urban myth that has been circulating for months,' said Justice Department spokeswoman Susan Dryden. 'The department has no information at this time to substantiate these widespread reports about Israeli art students involved in espionage.'"[65]

Confronted with the evidence, the denialists equate documented reports from reputable news sources with stories of alligators in the New York City sewer system. Faced with a leaked government document that reveals names, places, and military identification numbers, government spokesmen resort to characterizing the (so far unknown) leaker as a "disgruntled" DEA employee who single-handedly wrote the memo. We don't know what person or persons authored the DEA task force report on Israeli spy activity in the U.S. prior to 9/11, but certainly the 180 separate incidents documented in the memo were not reported by a single individual.

As the new revelations were met with a barrage of denials in Washington and Israeli consulates around the country, *Intelligence Online* editor Guillaume Dasquié stuck by his story. The FBI was engaging in sophistry, he said, when it denied that the "art students" had been arrested for carrying out espionage on behalf of a foreign power in the U.S.: all were expelled, the FBI piously averred, for routine visa violations. But, as Dasquié pointed out, that is precisely how a cover-up of spying by a "friendly" government would be accomplished: haul them into immigration court, get them out of the country quick—and no one's the wiser.

Ms. Dryden's arrogant dismissal of serious charges as an "urban myth" backfired. Denigrating your opponent when he has the goods on you is not a smart strategy. *Intelligence Online* threatened to publish the leaked government report in its entirety:

> "It seems irresponsible for us to publish it, but if the denials go on, we could put the report on our Internet site and in so doing possibly blacken the names of the people most exposed," the editor of the Intelligence Online site, Guillaume Dasquié, said…."The document we have in our possession details not only the identities of the members of this network, but also their activities in the Israeli army, and even their serial numbers in the intelligence services, their passport numbers and their validity, and their visas and their validity."[66]

Au contraire, Monsieur Dasquié, it was irresponsible to *refrain* from publishing it. We have a right to know the full context of the biggest terrorist attack in American history—an attack that signaled the start of a rapidly expanding war. The responsibility goes much higher than the son of an Israeli general and a few high-ranking intelligence officers—including responsibility for the ongoing cover-up. We've seen both the U.S. and Israeli governments going into full "spin" mode—the signal that a real panic was going on behind the scenes—one that provided those of us following this story with plenty of entertainment. There was, for example, the item in the South Florida *Sun-Sentinel* that reiterated the basic facts and reported that, in South Florida, these suspicious characters were employed by an outfit known as "Universal Art," with addresses in South Miami and Sunrise:

> On Wednesday, there was no sign of a company called Universal Art Inc., at 10873 NW 52nd St. in Sunrise. The address in Florida incorporation documents came back to a light industrial complex next to the Sawgrass Expressway and south of Commercial Boulevard. No one answered the door, and several occupants had not heard of the company. The company's officers, Yitzchak Shish and Chava Sagi, are not listed. They were not among those who were deported.[67]

The ripple effect caused by the French reports spread to the British media, and then went over the wire, reappearing in American media outlets—and forcing more of a response than the bland denials of the Israeli embassy. Daniel Pipes, well-known American Likudnik, strode forth to demolish this latest "urban myth," with an op ed piece in the *New York Post*, disingenuously entitled "An Israeli spy network in the United States?"[68]

Pipes' piece merely reiterated the allegations without refuting them—and without acknowledging the accumulating body of evidence. A disparaging tone is enough, he apparently believes, to dispel the cloud of suspicion that has hung over the Jewish state since the first stories about a massive round-up of Israelis in the U.S. began to appear. "American journalists," Pipes avers, "found not a shred of evidence to support the claim. More important, it met with wall-to-wall derision from the U.S. and Israeli governments." Cameron's reporting is summarily dismissed by Pipes. Also discounted is *Le Monde*, France's leading daily: "*Le Monde*'s account—with its crazy-quilt of unsourced allegations, drive-by innuendoes, and incoherent obscurities, but no hard facts—is nonsense."[69]

Here are a few of the facts that Pipes refused to mention:

- The U.S. government's National Counterintelligence Center put out an alert in March 2001 warning of persistent attempts by individuals identifying themselves as "art students" from Israel to penetrate U.S. government facilities.[70]

- As many as 200 were arrested in the months prior to and after 9/11.[71]

- The majority of these were members of the Israeli army's intelligence and counter-terrorism unit.[72]

- Some failed polygraph tests when asked if they were engaged in surveillance activities against the U.S.[73]

- Over a third resided in Florida. At least five were intercepted in the town of Hollywood, and two in Fort Lauderdale. Four of the five who diverted American Airlines flight 11, including ringleader Mohammed Atta, settled in Hollywood. Eight of the other terrorists lived in Delray Beach, just north of Fort Lauderdale.[74]

Pipes did not address any of these issues. He mentioned Gary Sick's "October surprise" allegations about Ronald Reagan, attacked CNN's controversial "Valley of Death" documentary, and rattled on about authors Gordon Thomas and Victor Ostrovsky—none of which have anything to do with the charge that the Israelis, as Carl Cameron put it, "may have gathered intelligence about the [9/11] attacks in advance, and not shared it."

It was a feeble, even a pathetic effort, one that seemed all the more threadbare in light of fresh revelations, detailed in an article written by Paul Rodriguez for *Insight*—a magazine published by the *Washington Times*, editorially a staunch supporter of Israel. Rodriguez provided yet another fascinating window into the underground world of Israeli covert action in America, and unearthed a few more "hard facts"—hard enough so that Pipes and his compadres would soon have to come up with a better spin than the "urban myth" gambit.[75]

Citing internal DEA documents and unnamed senior federal officials, Rodriguez confirmed Cameron's basic thesis: that, starting in 2000, organized teams of young Israelis who described themselves as "art students" descended on federal facilities, including military bases, ostensibly selling their paintings, and aggressively seeking access—not only to public buildings, but to the private homes of senior officials.

Rodriguez writes that the students "claimed to be from either the University of Jerusalem or the Bezalel Academy of Arts in Jerusalem." However, one news account that otherwise characterizes the whole affair as "murky" at best, and sprinkles the story liberally with denials from Anti-Defamation League honcho Abraham Foxman and several government officials, nonetheless informs us that "several of those questioned by investigators said they were students from Bezalel Academy of Art and Design. But Pnina Calpen, spokeswoman for the Israeli school, said no one named in the report was a student there in the last 10 years."[76]

Although these earnest young artists were supposedly peddling their own art, "information has been received which indicates the art is actually produced in China," Rodriguez says, citing the DEA's summary of the investigation:

> One report, "Suspicious Activities Involving Israeli Art Students at DEA Facilities," lists more than 180 documented-incident cases. Analysts tell *Insight* they appear to be attempts "to circumvent the access-control systems at DEA offices" and to capture personal information about private lives of DEA law-enforcement officers, such as where they live, what cars they drive and how they behave outside of their official offices. This was concluded, in part, based on photographs made of U.S. law officers and other materials seized by a variety of federal and local law-enforcement officers during searches.[77]

On September 14, 2001, New Jersey police moved in on Urban Moving Systems, a New Jersey company, and the residences of some of its employees, most of them Israelis. The raid was made in connection with the arrest of 5 men (initially reported as 3 men) all Israelis, eight hours after the World Trade Center was hit: they had been spotted cheering and jumping up and down in Liberty State Park as smoke from the burning WTC obscured the horizon. Witnesses reported them to the police, and identified their van with the logo of "Urban Moving Systems": they were picked up on Route 3, in East Rutherford, and detained. In an apparent follow-up raid, according to a September 14 report by WABC TV, New York, a dozen plainclothes cops, accompanied by bomb-sniffing dogs, entered the Urban Moving Systems warehouse "and began snapping pictures." "A few hours later, agents emerged from the building with more than 12 computer hard drives and files, piling them into the rear of a black Chevy Suburban."[78]

The [New Jersey] *Bergen Record* [11/15/01], in an account of the Weehawken raid, reports the following:

An employee of Urban Moving Systems, who would not give his name, said the majority of his co-workers are Israelis and were joking on the day of the attacks.

"I was in tears," the man said. "These guys were joking and that bothered me. These guys were like, 'Now America knows what we go through.'"[79]

There's your motive. We've heard this refrain repeated tirelessly since that time, echoed in the speeches of Ariel Sharon and his American amen corner. Speaking on the Christian Broadcast Network in the immediate aftermath of 9/11, Jerry Falwell told his rabidly pro-Israel "Christian Zionist" followers:

I talked this morning with Tom Rose publisher of the *Jerusalem Post*, and orthodox Jew, and he said, "Now America knows in a horrible way what Israel's been facing for 53 years at the hand of Arafat and other terrorists and radicals and barbarians."[80]

Appearing at a pro-Israel rally in Washington D.C., Bush administration ultra-hawk Paul Wolfowitz, the deputy secretary of defense, declared to cheering thousands:

Since September 11th, we Americans have one thing more in common with Israelis. On that day America was attacked by suicide bombers. At that moment every American understood what it was like to live in Jerusalem, or Netanya or Haifa. And since September 11th Americans now know why we must fight and win the war on terrorism.[81]

What a difference a terrorist attack on U.S. soil makes. Contrast this effusive declaration of unconditional support for Israel with the behavior of U.S. law enforcement agencies in the months prior to 9/11, when they picked up 60 Israelis posing as "art students." They rounded 120 more before the dust had settled over New York City, searching residences and interrogating the detainees—and with good reason. Rodriguez discovered:

> Besides federal law-enforcement incidents, DEA's I[nternal] S[ecurity] unit found that several military bases also had experienced unauthorized entries by some of the students, including two bases from which Stealth aircraft and other supersecret military units operate. Unauthorized photographing of military sites and civilian industrial complexes, such as petroleum-storage facilities, also was reported to the DEA, the documents show and interviews confirm.[82]

An "art project" that includes photographing super-secret military installations is properly described as espionage. While Rodriguez is careful to say there is no evidence that this pattern of suspicious activity was state-sponsored, the probability that these are graduates of the Mossad School of Art (summa cum laude) is certainly high. They seemed to be very well-organized, and quite single-minded, far above the level of any ordinary criminal gang. As Rodriguez put it:

> In virtually every incident of the many reported by the entire DEA field-office structure the pattern was similar: Students would attempt to enter secure buildings, take photographs, follow federal agents when they left buildings, show up at their homes, take pictures of their cars and circle their neighborhoods, visiting only their houses and then departing.[83]

Behind the bland denials, federal law enforcement officials were stunned. Rodriguez quotes one high-ranking official who exclaimed "it is a very alarming set of documents. This shows how serious DEA and Justice consider this activity." Another federal agent confides: "The higher-ups don't want to deal with this and neither does the FBI because it involves Israel." A Justice Department official tells Rodriguez: "We think there is something quite sinister here but are unable at this time to put our finger on it."[84]

The picture that emerges of a nation besieged gives us the vital context in which the horrific events of 9/11 occurred—a bold covert invasion of American soil by Israeli-sponsored spies.

Pipes and other would-be debunkers are trying to impugn the story's sources without bothering to dispute—or even refer to—the known facts. On the same day the Pipes' piece came out, the *Wall Street Journal*'s resident online "blogger," James Taranto, weighed in with his own spin on "the weird story of those Israeli 'art students'" "The 61-page DEA report suggests the Israelis' wanderings 'may well be an organized intelligence-gathering activity,'" he averred, "yet it mostly chronicles people selling overpriced paintings door to door."[85]

Taranto quoted government officials denying all and cited a few items from the DEA report selectively leaked to the Associated Press, "most of which sound utterly harmless." We are then treated to a two sentence description of a Dallas sighting torn out of a 60-page report: "Five people were selling art out of a van behind a small office complex that was closed for the holidays. A Euless, Texas, police officer found 40 to 50 pieces of art. 'Neither the frames nor the artwork appeared to be high quality, per the officer.'"[86]

However, even in this sanitized version of what the internal security task force discovered, we get the following item from St. Louis: "Suspected Palestinian or Middle Eastern art sellers were thought to be 'diagramming' the inside of a DEA building. Also, an agent said two people came to his house trying to sell art. 'What was unusual is that he watched them and they did not visit any other houses in the area,' the security alert said."[87]

More than a dozen Israeli "students" were rounded up in Kansas and Missouri in the wake of 9/11, and more than 50 throughout the Midwest.[88] In one Texas government building, according to KHOU-TV in Houston, they caught one of these phony "art students" wandering the halls with a floor plan of the building in hand.[89] Nonetheless, Pipes exclaims, "Shame, then, on those media outlets that contributed to this dangerous falsehood."[90]

The real shame is that the story of Israel's spy nest in the U.S. went nearly unreported for so long. It is telling that the "mainstream" media wouldn't touch this one with a ten-foot pole: it was left to Fox News, the brash young kid on the block, the relatively candid European media, and "alternative" news sources, such as Antiwar.com, to break the embargo on this vitally important story. The news, no longer centrally-planned and directed by a few self-appointed "gate-keepers," has been at least partially liberated, not only by the internet, but by the mindset that accompanies this technological breakthrough: one that challenges government propaganda and "spin" instead of reinforcing it.

In spite of the efforts of two governments, and a private lobby of not inconsiderable influence, to bury it, this story refused to die. Seven months after Carl Cameron broke the news of a vast Israeli underground in the U.S.—a spy apparatus that in many ways paralleled the Muslim terrorist network in the U.S.—it had come back to haunt them. From this point—mid-March 2002—on, the story would begin to play out and develop against the increasingly unconvincing denials of government officials and Israel's apologists, who could no longer airily dismiss it as an "urban myth."

3

The Story of the Century

By March, 2002, the story of Israel's extensive underground apparatus in the U.S.—and its key role in the events leading up to 9/11—was too big to be ignored, and too evident to be denied for much longer. *The Forward*, the oldest Jewish publication in the United States—a source unlikely to be biased against Israel—confirmed Cameron's core thesis:

> Despite angry denials by Israel and its American supporters, reports that Israel was conducting spying activities in the United States may have a grain of truth, *The Forward* has learned. However, far from pointing to Israeli spying against U.S. government and military facilities, as reported in Europe last week, the incidents in question appear to represent a case of Israelis in the United States spying on a common enemy, radical Islamic networks suspected of links to Middle East terrorism.[91]

The solid reporting done by Fox News, *Le Monde*, *Intelligence Online*, and *Insight* gives us a fairly clear outline of Israel's massive covert action operations in the U.S., which basically contained at least three known tentacles:

1. A national network of agents—the "art students"—specifically tasked with penetrating law enforcement agencies, such as the INS, the DEA, the FBI, as well as military facilities, such as Tinker Air Force Base.

2. A Florida-based operation, also designed to keep a watch on Al Qaeda, with cells incubating in California, and North Carolina.

3. The New Jersey-based "Urban Movers" cell, a Mossad front masquerading as a legitimate business, whose agenda, although shrouded in mystery, seems the most sinister—given the way it was discovered.

These are the laughing Israelis, mentioned in chapter one, who, hours after the hijackers struck the World Trade Center, were picked up by the police after onlookers reported them as jumping for joy at the sight of the twin towers burning. As smoke billowed up into the pellucid sky, obscuring the sun, they laughed and joked and took pictures of each other against a backdrop of unspeakable horror. Outraged witnesses called the cops, who swooped down and arrested them. These "Middle Eastern-looking men," as witnesses described them, turned out to be Israelis: they were found with box cutters in their van, $4,700 in cash hidden inside a sock, and multiple passports. The van was registered as the property of "Urban Moving Systems." Police interrogated them and transferred them to a maximum security facility. A raid on the Urban Moving Systems warehouse (whose owner, Dominik Suter, has since fled to Israel) yielded computers, documents, and other evidence.

In mid-March, *The Forward* reported the arrested Israelis were "subjected to an unusual number of polygraph tests and interrogated by a series of government agencies including the FBI's counterintelligence division, which by some reports remains convinced that Israel was conducting an intelligence operation." Furthermore:

> According to one former high-ranking American intelligence official, who asked not to be named, the FBI came to the conclusion at the end of its investigation that the five Israelis arrested in New Jersey last September were conducting a Mossad surveillance mission and that their employer, Urban Moving Systems of Weehawken, N.J., served as a front.[92]

Now that their spy nest had been exposed, and denials no longer worked, the Israelis were driven back to their second line of defense: Yes, we *were* watching Al Qaeda, "our common enemy," but, as *The Forward* was quick to add: "Sources emphasized that the release of all the Israelis under investigation indicates that they were cleared of any suspicion that they had prior knowledge of the September 11 attacks, as some anti-Israel media outlets have suggested."[93]

These "anti-Israel media outlets" are never named, but whom could they possible mean? The right-wing Fox News—which is now replacing CNN in Israel?[94] *Le Monde*? The day after the prominent French newspaper printed a story about the "Israeli art students," the same paper ran a commentary by the same author—back-pedaling furiously and raucously denouncing the "anti-Semitic fantasies" of those who think that the Israelis could have been involved in the events of 9/11.

Perhaps they mean *Intelligence Online*. But its editor, Guillaume Dasquie, has also pushed a theory that would seem to benefit the Israelis, and which echoes the neoconservative line that the whole conspiracy against America can be traced back to the government of Saudi Arabia.[95] This leaves the numerous newspapers and magazines, such as *Insight*, that reported on this story after it broke (for the second time): the Associated Press, the British papers, and most of the American media. But *Insight*, published by the staunchly pro-Israel *Washington Times*, can hardly be described as an "anti-Israel media outlet," and, as for the others—is *The Forward* saying that most of the American media is "anti-Israel"? By a process of elimination, tt seems likely they are referring to Antiwar.com, where the unusual pre-9/11 round-up of Israelis was first noted as significant evidence of an Israeli connection.[96]

Antiwar.com's policy stance is, in reality, not "anti-Israel," but merely pro-American—and pro-truth. We think the U.S. government should pursue a foreign policy that puts America first, not Israel, and believe the interests of the two longtime allies have radically diverged—as the story of the Israeli spy operation in the U.S. makes all too clear.

One interesting aspect of *The Forward* piece is that it raises the really fascinating question of what effect the Israeli spy scandal had on U.S.-Israeli relations—and to what extent it is a factor in setting the pace and direction of the extended diplomatic dance taking place over the Palestinian question:

"The resulting tensions between Washington and Jerusalem, sources told *The Forward*, arose not because of the operations' targets but because Israel reportedly violated a secret gentlemen's agreement between the two countries under which espionage on each other's soil is to be coordinated in advance."[97]

By revealing at least a small part of the truth, now, *The Forward* piece was an exercise in damage control. It was also, conceivably, a bit of payback to the Bush administration, which at that moment was putting pressure on the Israelis to let up on the Palestinians, and even endorsing a Palestinian state.[98]

The same issue of *The Forward* devotes a separate story, "FBI Probe Defuses Israeli Spying Rumors," to the "Israeli art students" aspect of the spy apparatus, and tries to paint a more equivocal picture. The piece starts off with denials by Israeli and U.S. government officials and ends with this dubious alibi: "A former senior U.S. intelligence official offered a different hypothesis. 'My guess and the one I heard from people in counterintelligence is that this could have been an Israeli training exercise, because they were all young and amateurish,' he said."[99]

Are we really expected to believe that the Israelis consider U.S. government and military facilities as fair game for target practice in their clandestine wargames? Surely this is more fantastic, and unlikely, than the straightforward and logical explanation: that the events described in the DEA report were indeed an Israeli covert action.

"Urban Moving Systems" was clearly a scam operation: the company was on several "blacklists" prepared by consumer advocate groups. Indeed, in researching this particular company, I was surprised to learn that a whole movement has grown up protesting the outright thievery of fly-by-night movers, many of them run by Israeli nationals.[100] The scam is to quote one price, and later demand more, in cash, while holding their victims' possessions hostage. When the employees of one such company, Advanced Moving Systems, in Florida, were arrested and charged with robbery and assault, the outraged response of the owner paralleled the protestations of Pipes and U.S. government officials that the "Israeli art student" spy operation was just an "urban myth" with anti-Semitic overtones. As the Milwaukee *Journal-Sentinel* reported: "'It's all against the Jews. The police are lying. They are corrupt,' said Zion Rokah, an Israeli national who owns Advanced Moving Systems in Sunrise, Fla., a suburb of Fort Lauderdale."[101]

Essentially the same charge is being made against U.S. law enforcement sources who leaked information on the Israeli "art students" spy ring to Fox News and other outlets: the police are lying, and, it is strongly implied, are anti-Semitic to boot. "Conspiracy theories are easier to kill than to bury," Pipes laments. "They haunt the fringes of the political spectrum, poisoning the political debate."

Pipes and his confreres have done their best to kill this story, but disdain for "conspiracy theories" hasn't been enough to bury it for the simple reason that facts, as Ronald Reagan famously observed, are stubborn things. The accumulated facts recorded in the DEA's 60-page report had been leaked, bit by bit, to various reporters, resulting in sporadic fits of media coverage, which Israel's professional apologists did their best to debunk. But the availability of the report in its entirety—it was posted on the internet at the end of March, 2002, complete with the names and ranks of government agents involved—dealt a knockout blow to the debunkers.[102]

According to the report, the Internal Security office of the Drug Enforcement Administration became aware of a systematic effort to gain access to offices and government personnel in January of 2001. An official security alert was issued, a month later, instructing agents to watch for and detain these "art students" as they tried to talk their way into the offices and homes of DEA personnel. Just how the "students" found the home addresses of a large number of government employees is what apparently shocked somnolent federal agencies into action.[103]

By the end of March, 2001, several law enforcement agencies were on the lookout for these students of Israeli "art," and 13 were arrested in Irving, Texas, on immigration charges, and detained. The detainees were interrogated, revealing that the two principals of the operation were Itay Simon and Michael Calmanovic (pp. 12-13, paragraphs 39-41). The former was identified as in charge of the overall operation by an unnamed Israeli, while the latter was tagged as the leader of the Texas operation. Calmanovic had rented a number of apartments at two apartment complexes, and the landlady at one of them said that the approximately 25 Israelis in five different apartments had hurriedly abandoned the place right after the first 13 were busted.

Calmanovic and Simon were tracked down to another apartment complex, Hidden Ridge Apartments, also in Irving, where they were interrupted in the process of making their escape (p. 15, paragraph 49). Simon told his interrogators that he "did 'classified work for the Israeli army.'" According to the report, "Simon refused to answer questions about his military service." Calmanovic stated that he was a recently discharged "electronic intercept operator for the Israeli military" (p. 15, paragraph 50).

Both were arrested on immigration charges, and held on $50,000 bond. "This bond was immediately posted," the report says, but we are not told by whom. In another case of arrested Israeli "art students," we are told who posted bail: one Ophir Baer, an employee of AMDOCS (p. 13, paragraph 42), an Israeli-based company fingered by Cameron and Rodriguez in their respective exposés of Israeli penetration of U.S. communications systems. The octopus, once rattled, became visible.

Reading this document is a strange experience. The cumulative effect of these dry-as-sand descriptions of incident after incident of attempted penetration of U.S. government offices and officials' homes is to instill, in the reader, an ominous sense of growing urgency. The plot-line, as it slowly develops, is clear by the time we get to page 17, paragraph 54: this section describes an encounter with yet more "discharged" Israeli special operations officers at Dallas Fort Worth airport, on their way to join their fellow "art students." One of them has a printed-out "read-me" file in his luggage with a reference to a file named "DEA Groups." By then, even the most skeptical reader is inclined to believe that these were no ordinary "art students." As the DEA report described them:

Most admit to serving in the Israeli military. This is not surprising given the mandatory military service require [sic] in Israel, however, a majority of those questioned has [sic] stated they served in military intelligence, electronic signal intercept, or explosive ordinance units. Some have been linked to high-ranking officials in the Israeli military. One was the son of a two-star general, one served as the bodyguard to the head of the Israeli Army, one served in a Patriot missile unit. That these people are now traveling in the U.S. selling art seems not to fit their background.[104]

The DEA was not alone in sounding the alarm. The report notes that, on March 23, 2001, the Office of National Drug Control Policy (ONDCP) issued a National Security Alert describing "the apparent attempts by Israeli nationals to learn about government personnel and office layouts." In St. Louis, they were caught "diagramming" the DEA building (p. 23, paragraph 71). At the Tampa District Office of the DEA, in March 2001, a group of these "students" was apprehended trying to enter a locked, unmarked office on the fifth floor of the building, which no ordinary member of the public would even realize is a DEA office. Included in the haul was one Hanan Serfaty, 24, who told his interrogators that he had served in the Israeli army between the ages of 18-21: "When questioned as to what he did between the ages of 21-24, he refused to answer" (p. 27, paragraph 80). Found in his possession: 51 deposit and withdrawal slips from various Florida banks, totaling $107,502 in deposits, and $86,000 in withdrawals. Pretty good money for an Israeli "art student."

One particularly telling incident took place on May 3, 2001. When Peer Segalovitz, 27, showed up at the DEA Orlando District Office, peddling his line about being an "Israeli art student," federal agents pounced on him, detaining and interrogating him for four hours. According to the DEA report: "[He] was untruthful about his reasoning to be in the U.S. for approximately the first three hours. Segalovitz finally admitted that he was one of approximately 30 Israeli art students who are currently in Florida. [He] would not admit what their purpose was in Florida, but did state that they were not here for legitimate means" (p. 31, paragraph 96).

This "art student" had been a platoon leader in the Israeli army; he and his men, Segalovitz told his interrogators, "specialized in demolition." He also begged the federal agents "not to divulge this information to Israel, because it would lead to his arrest in Israel." (The report adds an interesting detail: a car that had been parked outside the Orlando office as Segalovitz was being interviewed "sped away" when approached.)

In Richmond, Virginia, one of the Israeli "students" tried to enter the DEA District Office surreptitiously, and was apprehended. Tinker Air Force Base, in Oklahoma City, was also targeted: after an alert was issued, four spies were nabbed in the vicinity, and arrested. Volk Field Air National Guard Base, in Camp Douglas, Wisconsin, saw an incursion by two young Israeli nationals, who were observed photographing the facilities and subsequently taken into custody. Both were asked if they had been involved in selling artwork in the U.S., and one, Gal Kantor, "became very upset over this, and questioned [why] they were being asked about that," according to the report. "Sgt. Kurt Moore of Volk Field stated that when asked about the art sales, Kantor's whole demeanor changed, and he became uncooperative."

Both "students" asked to telephone the Israeli embassy, no doubt to receive further orders. But what were their *original* orders? With the U.S. government's own report made public, in full, there was no longer any doubt as to the spy ring's existence. The question now became: what was its purpose?

The primary mission of any spy is surveillance—and the persistent attempts to enter offices and residences of U.S. government employees could point to an effort to plant bugging devices, as well as provide photographic and other intelligence on the physical layout of government and military facilities. Another purpose, however, was more focused. As John Sugg points out in his excellent article published in the Tampa [Florida] *Weekly Planet*: "Many of the apparent [Israeli] operatives had set up shop at addresses only stones' throws from Arabs in San Diego, Little Rock, Irving, Texas, and in South Florida. The *Planet* also has obtained a watch list of mostly Arabs under scrutiny by the U.S. government. The addresses of many correspond to the specific areas where the Israelis established bases."[105]

The question of foreknowledge of the 9/11 attack has been the subject of several unfortunate conspiracy theories—unfortunate in the sense that they discredit any real challenge to the "official" non-story. The most infamous is the one advanced by former congresswoman Cynthia McKinney, who seems to believe that George W. Bush knew all about the terrorist attacks in advance, and deliberately let 9/11 happen because "persons close to this administration are poised to make huge profits off America's new war."[106] She offered no evidence for her claim, yet insisted on a congressional investigation.

Everybody is using 9/11 to promote their own "smelly little orthodoxies," as Orwell described the mindset of the ideologues of his time. Just as the neoconservatives are using 9/11 to promote their program of war, and yet more war, the loonier factions of the left are seizing the moment to demonstrate, to their own satisfaction if no one else's, that "Bush knew," and that the Americans, in effect, bombed themselves.

The neocons are far more dangerous, because their hands are on the levers of power, or close enough. But the threat posed by McKinney is equally pernicious, because it closes off the possibility of the public ever discovering the truth about 9/11.

Initially, the American public was too anesthetized by daily announcements of imminent terrorist strike to question the official story. As far as the national "mainstream" media was concerned, Carl Cameron's reporting had fallen down an Orwellian memory hole. *Jane's Intelligence Digest* put it this way: "It is rather strange that the U.S. media seems to be ignoring what may well be the most explosive story since the 11 September attacks—the alleged break-up of a major Israeli espionage operation in the U.S.A."[107]

But this selective blindness is not really all that strange, considering the traditional cowardice of the mainstream print and broadcast media when it comes to offending two of the most powerful constituencies in the business of journalism: government officials and the pro-Israel lobby. The former because they are, after all, the source of so much news; the latter because of their increasingly militant tactics when it comes to journalism that puts Israel in a bad light. In the age of the internet, however, where advertising matters less and persistence (along with timeliness) is what counts, the story of the century was bound to get out, and so it finally did—in a spectacular way—on Salon.com.

The central thesis of Christopher Ketcham's stunning piece was given this sub-head: "For almost two years, hundreds of young Israelis falsely claiming to be art students haunted federal offices—in particular, the DEA. No one knows why—and no one seems to want to find out."[108]

Particularly disturbing to law enforcement, according to Ketcham's sources, was the ability of the Israelis to detect unmarked government offices, "leading authorities to suspect that information had been gathered from prior surveillance or perhaps electronically, from credit cards and other sources." He notes the geographic congruence of the Israeli "artists" and Mohammed Atta's psychotic death cult, concentrated particularly in South Florida. By Ketcham's count, at least three separate federal "alerts" from different agencies went out, and, before the secret war was over, "some 140 Israeli nationals were detained or arrested between March 2001 and September 11, 2001, and some 60 afterward." The University of Jerusalem, where many claimed to be enrolled, turned out to be nonexistent, and their other alleged alma mater—Bezalel Academy of Arts and Design in Jerusalem—had never heard of any of them.

This is "a blockbuster tale," writes Ketcham, "albeit a bizarre and cryptic one, full of indeterminate leads and fascinating implications and ambiguous answers: 'Like a good Clancy novel,' as one observer put it."

Actually, much more like a novel by Phillip K. Dick, the science fiction writer whose subversive imagination interacted with a kaleidoscopic paranoia in unique and often disturbing ways. Indeed, Ketcham's narrative has a novelistic feel, and all the major elements of popular fiction: high drama, espionage, and even sex: "The females among them were invariably described as 'very attractive'—'blondes in tight shorts or jeans, real lookers,' as one DEA agent put it to Salon. 'They were flirty, flipping the hair, looking at you, smiling. 'Hey, how are you? Let me show you this.' Everything a woman would do if she wanted to get something out of you."

Ketcham credits the earliest news reports of the Israeli incursion to an October 1, 2001, investigative report by Anna Werner, of Houston's KHOU-TV, detailing, in Werner's words, a "curious pattern of behavior" by intruders with "Middle Eastern looks" claiming to be Israeli art students. The DEA Houston headquarters, as well as the Leland Federal Building, had been targeted, and one had been found wandering the halls of the Earle Cabell Federal Building in Dallas "with a floor plan of the site" in hand. Werner reported similar incidents at "36 sensitive Department of Defense sites." She quotes a former Defense Department analyst as saying: ""One defense site you can explain. Thirty-six? That's a pattern."

But Werner got it wrong: she thought they were Arabs masquerading as Israelis, possibly a terrorist group "scouting out potential targets and…looking for targets that would be vulnerable." Ketcham avers that "post-9/11, this should have been the opening thrust in an orgy of coverage, and the scoop of a lifetime for Werner." But it never happened: "The story died on the vine" because "no one followed up." Cameron's four-part series—although "none of it was necessarily conclusive"—sank like a stone in similar manner, "and the scuttlebutt in major newsrooms was that Cameron's sources—all anonymous—were promulgating a fantasy."

According to Ketcham, reporters from the *New York Times* and the *Washington Post* expected "their go-to people" in law enforcement and intelligence to confirm the story, and when it was met with derision wrote it off. But behind the scenes, Ketcham reports, the U.S. government was taking Cameron dead seriously. An internal DEA memo specifically mentioning the Fox News story "warns of security breaches in DEA telecommunications by unauthorized 'foreign nationals'—and cites an Israeli-owned firm with which the DEA contracted for wiretap equipment—breaches that could have accounted for the access that the 'art students' apparently had to the home addresses of agents."

Comverse/Infosys, now called Verint Systems, is a company that describes itself as "a global organization providing analytic software solutions for communications interception, digital video security and surveillance, and enterprise business intelligence. We generate actionable intelligence through the collection, retention and analysis of voice, fax, video, email, Internet and data transmissions from multiple types of communications." As a longtime leader of the Military Industrial Complex, the newly-reconstituted and re-named Verint has recently contracted with VeriSign, which runs the internet registry and markets digital verification services, to enable the communications industry to come into compliance with the U.S. "PATRIOT" Act. A VeriSign press release touted its latest product as

> A one-stop, turnkey solution for telecom carriers facing the June 30, 2002 deadline for compliance with CALEA—the Communications Assistance for Law Enforcement Act. The FCC's 1994 CALEA mandate, recently moved along by passage of the U.S.A Patriot Act, requires telecom service providers to support the ability of law enforcement agencies to conduct lawfully authorized electronic surveillance of call content and call data. Before VeriSign's solution, compliance required potentially costly new equipment or system upgrades by the carrier, as well as maintaining special security staff and facilities. After June 30, non-compliant carriers could face a fine of $10,000 per day for each intercept request from a law enforcement agency.[109]

And Verint has the software: "Using Verint Systems' STAR-GATETM, a series of solutions that connect switching systems and provide the means to access and deliver intercepted communications content and call data to law enforcement agencies, VeriSign offers a streamlined solution..."[110]

VeriSign has come up with a snappy slogan to market its products in the security-conscious post-9/11 era: "Trust is the Foundation of Every Human Relationship." But the system is not to be trusted; it is full of holes, as veterans of law enforcement have been complaining for years, and as the Dutch recently discovered. *c't*, a Dutch hi-tech magazine, reports a similar breach in their security systems: "According to anonymous sources within the Dutch intelligence community, all tapping equipment of the Dutch intelligence services and half the tapping equipment of the national police force, is insecure and is leaking information to Israel.... The discussion focuses on the tapping installations for telephony and internet delivered to the government in the last few years by the Israeli company Verint."[111]

According to the magazine's sources in Dutch law enforcement and among computer experts, Comverse struck a deal with the Dutch in which the Israelis were given full access to all material intercepted by Dutch authorities, in return for the Comverse computer system at bargain basement prices. Except the Comverse product wound up being more expensive than any of the competitor bids, due to "maintenance" costs—and not just in monetary terms. "Since the leaks seem to be disguised as maintenance," the magazine points out, "one could say that the Dutch government is actually paying the cost of foreign intelligence against the Dutch state."[112]

In the Netherlands, as in the U.S., veteran law enforcement officials were the first to sound the alarm. In an October 10 [2002] letter to hi-tech vendors, the Council of Chiefs of Police ("raad van hoofdcommissarissen") cited "the situation in the U.S." as a cause for "concern" about their own security systems.

"Trust is the Foundation of Every Human Relationship"—but not of the relations between nations and their respective governments, especially in the intelligence-gathering realm. Like Cameron, Ketcham understands this, and sees, also, that the trust supposedly binding two close allies may be entirely one-sided.

Rather than accept the DEA report as gospel, Ketcham went back and interviewed some of the agents involved: "Salon contacted more than a half-dozen agents identified in the memo. One agent said she had been visited six times at her home by 'art students.' None of the agents wished to be named, and very few were willing to speak at length, but all confirmed the veracity of the information."

Although quick to point out "obvious holes in the official story," Ketcham is cautious to the point of timidity in drawing any conclusions: he writes that both *Le Monde* and *Intelligence Online* "jumped the gun" and drew conclusions unsupported by the facts.

But what if Anna Werner had been right, and these "Middle Eastern-looking" and definitely suspicious "art students" had been, let's say, Iraqis, or some other Middle Eastern Arab nationality—would it have been "jumping the gun" to posit a terrorist operation?

What *Insight* magazine describes as "the investigators' take on this" is the only logical conclusion: "What were these 'students' doing going around accessing buildings without authorization, tracking undercover cops to their homes—if not for some sort of intel mission? It's sort of a mind-fuck scenario, if one were to believe this was a conspiracy by a foreign intel source and/or a bunch of nutty 'kids' fucking around just to see how far they could push the envelope—which they seem to have pushed pretty damn far, given the page after page after page of intrusions and snooping alleged."[113]

While "nutty kids" do not suddenly up and decide to systematically breach security perimeters at a wide range of U.S. government and military facilities, the idea that this Israeli operation was some sort of "mindfuck" is more plausible. Keeping in mind the timeframe in which these intrusions occurred—the immediate period prior to 9/11—in retrospect their purpose may have been to sow confusion and divert attention away from something else that was going on.

Ketcham goes on at length about all the reasons why allegations of Israeli spying in the U.S. might be a particularly sensitive matter, as far as journalists and government officials are concerned, bitterly detailing efforts by pro-Israel pressure groups to spike this story. He cites Alex Safian, associate director of CAMERA (Committee for Accuracy in Middle East Reporting in America), as saying that "Jewish-Israeli groups" were "having conversations" with Fox News about Cameron's breakthrough four-part exposé. Safian slimes Cameron as an anti-Semite—not because of anything he reported, but because of where he was brought up: "I think Fox has always been fair to Israel in its reporting," said Safian—meaning that Fox has always been vehemently pro-Israel—but "I think it's just Cameron who has something, personally, about Israel. He was brought up in the Middle East. Maybe that has something to do with it. Maybe he's very sympathetic to the Arab side. One could ask."[114]

Confronted with Safian's smear, Cameron, for his part, could hardly believe his ears. Ketcham reports him as saying: "I'm speechless. I spent several years in Iran growing up because my father was an archaeologist there. That makes me anti-Israel?"

While Cameron stoutly maintains that he came under no pressure whatsoever, either from government officials or Fox News management, Ketcham tells a different story. He notes that Le Monde's request for a copy of the Cameron tapes was met with stonewalling: Fox denies even receiving such a request. In addition to those "conversations" between Israel's amen corner and Fox, Ketcham also points to the mysterious disappearance of the Cameron story from Fox's website. Normally a story stays up for a few weeks, but in this case it was deleted after four days, and, instead of being consigned to the for-pay archives, anyone who clicked on the link was told "this story no longer exists." Obviously that is what some people were fervently hoping.

Much of Ketcham's piece is devoted to reiterating what others have written and reported, but he does introduce a brand new element, one that is startling, and yet so plausible that it succeeds in unraveling this mystery almost to its core. As Ketcham tells it:

> The extreme sensitivity of the Israeli art student story in government circles was made clear to this reporter when, in the midst of my inquiries at DEA and elsewhere, I was told by a source that some unknown party had checked my records and background. He proved it by mentioning a job I had briefly held many years ago that virtually no one outside my family knew about. Shortly after this, I received a call from an individual who identified himself only by the code name Stability. Stability said he was referred to me from "someone in Washington." That someone turned out to be a veteran D.C. correspondent who has close sources in the CIA and the FBI and who verified that Stability was a high-level intelligence agent who had been following the art student matter from the inside.[115]

Stability, though "guarded" at first, gradually becomes more voluble, and tells Ketchan that "patriots" in law enforcement—those who talked to Cameron, presumably, and leaked the DEA report—"have taken a lot of heat on this." But "typically," says Stability, "patriots are dead."

Whether he means that literally or figuratively is left to the readers' imagination, but, in any case, the government has retaliated in other ways against federal agents responsible for leaking the Israeli spy memo: "Half a dozen agents have been polygraphed several times over, computers have been seized, desks have been searched." According to Ketcham's source, the existence of an Israeli covert operation prior to the horrific events of 9/11 is "indisputable." "But to what end?" asks Ketcham. "What was the value? What was to be gained?" Stability has no answer:

"'Unknown, unknown,' Stability said. 'You could be anywhere from D.C. to daylight on that one. Even on our side, you have to take all the stuff and draw it all out and clean out all the chaff. I will tell you that from those who are working ground zero [on this case], it is a difficult puzzle to put together, and it is not complete by any means.' Even the spooks are baffled; they have no answers."[116]

Stability's agnosticism is no way to end an article, however, and Ketcham lists four possible scenarios that would explain the Israeli "art student" mystery:

1. It was a drug gang operation. This is based on the premise that the Israelis' efforts seemed directed primarily at penetrating the DEA. Although Ketcham seems to be disdaining this possibility, his method of doing so is a curious one. He lists a panoply of perfectly credible motivations for a drug gang to pull off such an operation:

In the annals of crime chutzpah, for drug dealers to brazenly approach drug agents in their homes and offices may represent the all-time world record. And what conceivable useful intelligence could they gather that would be worth the risk? Were the tee-heeing tight-sweatered Israeli babes pulling some kind of Mata Hari stunt, seducing paunchy middle-aged DEA boys and beguiling them into loose-lipped info sharing?[117]

It sounds plausible, except for a few things not mentioned by Ketcham. For example: why would a drug gang be interested in monitoring military facilities, such as Tinker Air Force Base? And why is the possibility of an alliance of Israeli intelligence and the Israeli Mafia in the U.S. never broached? Intelligence agencies often deal with people whose moral sense is not highly developed, and certainly this can't be ruled out in the case of the Mossad, well-known for methods some would call unscrupulous, and others "efficient."

2.   They really *were* art students. This is dismissed as unlikely, considering that the "art schools" they claimed to be from either did not exist, or else had no record of their attendance.

3.   It was espionage—but "this doesn't make much sense," according to Ketcham. Why, after all, would the Mossad go barging into U.S. government offices and sensitive defense facilities in such an obvious way?

On the other hand, Ketcham fails to consider that it would be a good strategy precisely *because* of this objection. The sheer boldness of such a plan, a frontal assault from where it is least expected, would give the Israelis enough time to accomplish their objectives—whatever those might be. This points to and supports Ketcham's final scenario,

4.   It was a covert operation designed to throw off our own intelligence agencies. This appears to answer the above question. If the operation was conspicuous, then that was the whole point. Stability says to Ketcham:

It was a noisy operation. Did you ever see *Victor/Victoria*? It was about a woman playing a man playing a woman. Perhaps you should think about this from that aspect and ask yourself if you wanted to have something that was in your face, that didn't make sense, that couldn't possibly be them....Think of it this way: How could the experts think this could actually be something of any value? Wouldn't they dismiss what they were seeing?[118]

Now we're entering "truly dark territory," warns Ketcham, and the reader is inclined to agree. All the while maintaining his agnosticism, Ketcham outlines Stability's basic theory:

> Israeli agents wanted, let's say, to monitor al-Qaida members in Florida and other states. But they feared detection. So to provide cover, and also to create a dizzyingly Byzantine story that would confuse the situation, Israeli intel flooded areas of real operations with these bumbling "art students"—who were told to deliberately stake out DEA agents.[119]

Isn't this precisely the big complaint of the intelligence community, the problem the centralization of information embodied in the "Homeland Security" concept is supposedly designed to correct? What let the hijackers go undetected for years wasn't incompetence, or worse, agency heads, elected officials, and the "experts" tell us, it was "information overload." There was too much information coming in too fast, and no way to collate and organize it into a useful form. Certainly the "Victor/Victoria" thesis fits in neatly with this very plausible, albeit somewhat self-exculpatory analysis.

Ketcham ends his piece as an agnostic. The mystery is still protected at its core: "I nudged Stability on the obvious implication of the 'Victor/Victoria' scenario: If this was a ruse, a decoy to conceal another operation, what was that other operation? 'Unknown,' Stability said."

Unknown, but not unknowable, given new information since made available. What would be the point of someone trying to divert the attention of U.S. intelligence and law enforcement agencies in the period leading up to 9/11? The answer is made plain by a discovery made after Kecham's piece was published—documentary evidence that the U.S. government has uncovered links between suspected Israeli agents and the 9/11 terrorists and their supporters.

4

Smoldering Gun

Once the *Salon* story was published, the old standby line—"Move along, there's nothing to see here"—wasn't working that well anymore, and the debunkers were in retreat. The suspicion of an Israeli connection to the events of 9/11 had suddenly moved out of the realm of "conspiracy sites," and into the liberal-left audience catered to by Salon. Not only that, but Ketcham's piece generated a great deal of online discussion. The Israeli newspaper *Ha'aretz* wrote:

> It could be the biggest espionage scandal of the century, or the greatest journalistic non starter in many a decade, but it's clear that the story of the Israeli art students in New York—dozens of alleged spies living in the United States—refuses to die down. Anyone who believes the story says that everything is accurately documented and confirmed, and that only a conspiracy on the part of the U.S. administration—which is desperate to keep the affair quiet, partly out of shame and partly because of its warm relations with Israel—is keeping the affair out of the spotlight of public discussion. Those who repudiate the affair say it is baseless, just another unfounded urban legend that has taken on a life of its own on various marginal Internet sites. The most recent mention of the affair came last week in the highly respected Internet magazine, Salon.com, which recapped the main points of the scandal and even added some new details of its own.[120]

In spite of the Israelis' denials, the story, wrote *Ha'aretz*, "is alive and kicking." Online discussion of the Israeli "art students" story suddenly took on a reasonable tone,[121] and people who used to dismiss it out of hand began to reconsider. *The American Prospect*, journal of the Respectable Left, commented: "This immense investigative report by Christopher Ketcham on the 'Israeli art students' mystery, just published in Salon, is an absolute must read. Tapped, like everyone else, thought the allegations concerning an Israeli spy ring were off the reservation. Now we can't be so sure, and the information in Ketcham's story simply demands a serious response both from the media (which has neglected this matter) and from the U.S. government."[122]

The wall of silence surrounding the "art students" mystery had been breached. It was time for the debunkers to give a little ground, while shoring up their inner defenses. But would-be debunkers had a problem, and it was much bigger than the exposure of the "art students" as probable Israeli agents. While there was no direct connection between the activities detailed in the DEA report and 9/11, apart from Stability's speculation that this might have been a planned diversion, the Achilles heel of this operation was its New Jersey-based cell—which had been exposed in the hours after the World Trade Center was hit.

The five young Israeli men detained by police had been acting suspiciously, laughing and seeming to jump for joy as the World Trade Center burned. Outraged witnesses described them as "Middle Eastern-looking," and the police soon interrupted their celebration. What they found in the search of their van was so incriminating that they were detained, interrogated for hours, and transferred to a maximum security facility.

Their van, registered to Urban Moving Systems, was impounded, and two days later the authorities moved in on the Urban Moving Systems warehouse. A report broadcast by WABC-TV described the raid:

> Officers had visited the warehouse Tuesday night, surveying it from the outside with bomb-sniffing dogs, then went inside on Thursday, the *Star-Ledger* of Newark reported.[123] About a dozen plainclothes officers, including investigators from the Bergen County Sheriff's Department, entered Urban Moving Systems at about 8 p.m. and began snapping pictures.... A few hours later, agents emerged from the building with more than 12 computer hard drives and files, piling them into the rear of a black Chevy Suburban, the newspaper reported. Business owner Dominik Suter, who was at the building when agents searched it, refused to comment.[124]

Suter's lawyer, Jay Hamill of Jersey City, claimed that "to the best of my knowledge, my client Urban Moving Systems and Dominik Suter are not targets" of the terrorism investigation. "This is an informational situation. We're cooperating completely and have objected to nothing they've requested."[125]

According to the New Jersey Division of Consumer Affairs, "on or about September 14, 2001, Suter departed from the United States and left no one acting as an agent for Urban [Moving Systems]."[126] His destination was Israel, and since then he has taken the same stance he did the day the cops raided his spy nest: no comment.[127]

The widespread reports on the Israeli "art student" affair were the least of the debunkers' problems. In Weehawken, the soft underbelly of Israel's spy network in the U.S. had been exposed at its most vulnerable point—and it was only a matter of time before some enterprising reporter connected the dots. A tactical retreat was in order, one that would put the right "spin" on the situation: that the five detained Israelis, subjected to numerous polygraph tests and interrogated for as much as 16 hours at a stretch,[128] were probably Israeli intelligence agents—but they had no connection to, and certainly no foreknowledge of, what happened on 9/11.

On June 21, 2002, the ABC News program *20/20* broadcast "The White Van," which was intended, as anchorperson Barbara Walters intoned at the end, to "put all these rumors to rest." Yet the show opened with an interview with a woman who had spotted the joyous Israelis from her highrise as they laughed and cheered while the twin towers burned: it was she who had reported them to the police. The woman, who would identify herself only as "Maria," had a baffled look on her face as she described the behavior of the young Israelis: "They were like happy, you know…They didn't look shocked to me. I thought it was very strange."[129]

But Israela Marmari, the mother of one of the detainees, has a different perspective: "They are good boys. They are so innocent. My son was in shock [after his arrest]. He said, 'Mommy, I can't believe it. We are Israeli and live with terror every day. How could anybody believe that Israelis could do anything like this?'"[130]

Omer Marmari was "in shock" after his arrest—but *not* after terrorists drove two airliners into the World Trade Center. Far from benumbed, from the eyewitness account of observers such as "Maria," he and his co-workers were ecstatic.

Much of ABC's report confirms the contention that there was indeed, as Carl Cameron put it, a "vast Israeli spy operation" in the U.S. in full operational mode prior to 9/11, engaged in watching the pro-Arab support network that operates in many major American cities. This report amounted to the Israelis' second line of defense, which basically boils down to this: the five detainees *were* Israeli spies, but they were here defending Israel's interests and had no pre-knowledge of 9/11. In the process of spinning this new rationale, however, we have a series of damning admissions, as spun by ABC terrorism expert Vince Cannistraro, a former chief of operations for counterterrorism with the CIA.

The arrested men's names, we learn, were found in a search of a national intelligence database. We are also told by Cannistraro that Urban Moving Systems was probably a Mossad front. The purpose of this spy nest, we are told in a reassuring tone, was "launching an intelligence operation against radical Islamists in the area, particularly in the New Jersey-New York area."

"Under this scenario," says Cannistraro, "the alleged spying operation was not aimed against the United States, but at penetrating or monitoring radical fund-raising and support networks in Muslim communities like Paterson, N.J., which was one of the places where several of the hijackers lived in the months prior to Sept. 11."

The problem with this fallback story is that penetrating or monitoring New Jersey Muslims and having foreknowledge of 9/11 are not mutually exclusive. Indeed, such surveillance—to the degree it was successful—would have increased the likelihood that the Israelis would gain some knowledge of the 9/11 plot. If not all the details, at least a strong indication that 9/11 was bound to be a special day—one they would celebrate, shamelessly and carelessly, in full sight of others, unable to restrain their joy at the sight of the WTC emitting a black cloud over Manhattan.

A September 14 *New York Times* round-up of the nationwide investigation into the terrorist attacks described the mood of the Israelis as they watched the disaster unfold:

> In New Jersey, where officials believe that the hijackers received assistance from accomplices, Sherri Evanina, a spokeswoman for the FBI in Newark... said witnesses had reported seeing the men celebrating the attack on the World Trade Center earlier in the day in Union City. "They were seen leaving the location after they were celebrating," Agent Evanina said. "They were watching the entire event from their location."[131]

If the best comedy is unintentional, then "The White Van" is chock full of yucks: "For the FBI, deciphering the truth from the five Israelis proved to be difficult. One of them, Paul Kurzberg, refused to take a lie-detector test for 10 weeks—then failed it, according to his lawyer. Another of his lawyers told us Kurzberg had been reluctant to take the test because he had once worked for Israeli intelligence in another country."[132]

For the FBI, it seems, deciphering anything that isn't completely spelled out for them is well nigh impossible. "Despite the denials," *20/20* reports, "sources tell ABC News there is still debate within the FBI over whether or not the young men were spies." As John Stossel, Barbara Walters' *20/20* colleague, ceaselessly reiterates: "Gimme a *break!*"

Why, in this case, is it so hard for the FBI to discover the truth—when they're being practically hit over the head with it? It's pathetic, really, to contemplate the utter cluelessness of America's chief federal law enforcement agency, and the reporters who take their denials seriously.

ABC reporter John Miller babbles on: "Many U.S. government officials" concede the Urban Movers were Mossad spies, in the area on a specific mission, but don't worry, folks, because the FBI is telling us "To date, this investigation has not identified anybody who in this country had pre-knowledge of the events of 9/11." Note the curiously tentative nature of this disclaimer: "to date."

The *20/20* technique is merely to drag Cannistraro out, who references mysterious "sources" to conclude that those lost Israelis were just having some good clean fun that day, protecting Israel against terrorism (in New Jersey!). Says Cannistraro: "The investigation, at the end of the day, after all the polygraphs, all of the field work, all the cross-checking, the intelligence work, concluded that they probably did not have advance knowledge of 9/11."

Aside from this singularly unconvincing argument from authority, one has to ask: is "probably not" a good enough answer when we're asking whether Israel had foreknowledge of 9/11, and somehow failed to let us in on the secret?

The tale of the White Van, as told by *20/20*, raises more questions than it settles. What about those polygraphs? Kurzberg failed his. We are told that some of the Israeli detainees "were given as many as seven lie-detector tests." Why so many? The five were detained for over two months, a month of it in solitary confinement, time and opportunity enough for an awful lot of questions.

The intrepid reporters over at *20/20* went to a lot of trouble to check out this story. They tracked down one of the original witnesses, went all the way to Israel to hear the young Israelis' denials, and hauled out ABC's highly-paid "expert" to spin away the obvious. Yet Barbara Walters and her babbling yes-man left out the entire context of the larger Israeli spy story, as uncovered by Carl Cameron, and since widely reported both here and abroad. They failed also to do the basic research that would have demanded only a trip to their local library. There they might have read this astonishing story that appeared in the [September 12, 2001] *Bergen Record*:

> [S]ources close to the investigation said they found other evidence linking the men to the bombing plot. "There are maps of the city in the car with certain places highlighted," the source said. "It looked like they're hooked in with this. It looked like they knew what was going to happen when they were at Liberty State Park."[133]

So it wasn't just the expression on their faces as they watched the World Trade Center go down: there was actual physical evidence, as well as the testimony of a police insider, linking them to the attacks.

More documentary evidence of the Israeli connection to 9/11 came to light with the emergence of the U.S. government's own list of terrorist suspects, two versions of which cryptome.com obtained and posted on September 11, 2002, with the following information as to their provenance: "A Finnish list of FBI terrorist suspects, dated 3 October 2001, first published about six months ago, may be compared to a similar list published on an Italian site, dated 22 May 2002. The two lists have many of the same names but a fair number of names are unique to each, and the Finnish list provides a 'function' and ID for each suspect."[134]

There are also other differences. The Italian document—originally posted on the website of the Associazione Italiana per il Factoring (the Italian industry association), and now blocked[135]—indicates that this is an official U.S. government circular originating with the FBI and distributed to various Italian financial institutions in an effort to trace the terrorist trail. All names on the Finnish list are Arabic. The Italian version, however, has a number of American names as well, one Frenchman, and there is our old friend Dominik Suter, listed right between Eyad Suleiman, a native of Kuwait, and Sheikh Amed Salim Swedan, a Kenyan. Three addresses are listed for Suter—28 Harlow Crescent Road, Fair Lawn NJ; 312 Pavonia Avenue, Jersey City, NJ; and 15000 Dickens, Suite 11, Sherman Oaks CA—along with his Social Security number (129-78-0926), and his year of birth (1970). Unlike most of the others, however, his nationality is not given.

Also included is Ornit Levinson, alias Ornit Suter, with the same three addresses listed, born 1970, Social Security number: 122-78-0232. Her nationality is also omitted. When the Urban Moving Systems warehouse was raided, one newspaper account reported that "a woman answering the telephone at Suter's home acknowledged he owned the company but refused to comment further. She also declined to identify herself."[136] Perhaps the FBI terrorist suspect list has done that for us.

The inclusion of the Suters on an official list of terrorist suspects should silence for good those who dismiss the Israeli connection to 9/11 as a "myth," urban or otherwise. In fingering Suter and his "Urban Moving Systems" front as suspects in the terrorist investigation, I am merely reflecting what is apparently the de facto view of the FBI, in spite of its public statements.[137]

On that list, along with Mohammed Atta, and Zacarias Moussaoui, are not only the Suters, but also at least five other Americans—or, at least, non-Arabs with U.S. addresses—and a number of American businesses. It is no longer possible to deny that the U.S. government believes at least two Israeli nationals had some connection to the events leading up to 9/11.

The President of the United States has unequivocally stated that any nation "harboring terrorists" can expect to feel American wrath. On September 14, 2001, Congress passed a joint resolution, authorizing the President to "use all necessary and appropriate force against those nations, organizations, or persons he determines planned, authorized, committed, or aided the terrorist attacks that occurred on September 11, 2001, or harbored such organizations or persons."

Mr. Suter, who currently resides in Israel, has yet to be extradited to the U.S. Nor has there been any public indication that an extradition request has been made.

The presence of the Suters on the FBI's list of terrorist suspects is a key piece of evidence. Another important piece of the puzzle is an article by Oliver Schröm in *Die Zeit*, a German weekly, entitled: "Next Door to Mohammed Atta."[138]

Schröm reiterates the tale of the Israeli "art students" with a plethora of new details that fill in the story of Israel's secret war against the U.S. He notes that "American law enforcement agencies had earlier learned that a noticeably large number of Israeli students had applied for jobs at software development and technology firms that primarily served government agencies." Schröm not only confirms what Carl Cameron had first reported about the extent of Israeli penetration of security communications systems, but also debunks the canard, spread by Israel's amen corner, that the DEA report documenting the Israeli spy ring was just the work of a single "disgruntled" employee: "The obvious suspicion," wrote Schröm, "was that the young Israelis were members of a spy ring. A specially formed task force, consisting of employees of the DEA, INS and Office of Security Programs, looked into the matter."[139]

Compiled in the summer of 2001, the authors of the report must have known that any sensitive security matter involving Israel would likely meet resistance in Washington. They were no doubt unsurprised when the whole matter was quashed and the report suppressed at the top; remember what "Stability" said about agents having their computers, offices, and homes searched after the findings of the inter-agency task force were leaked. Why did they risk their careers, and perhaps even being brought up on charges? The answer is: 9/11. In all the information that was released about the hijackers, what must have struck them was the geography of the terrorist plot: the hijackers' cells in Phoenix, Arizona, Miami and Hollywood, Florida, paralleled nests of suspected Israeli spies. As Schröm puts it:

Not until after the attacks of September 11 did the consequences of the spy ring become clear. Apparently the agents were not interested in military or industrial facilities, but were shadowing a number of suspects, who were later involved in the terrorist attacks against the U.S. According to a report of the French intelligence agency that *Die Zeit* examined, "according to the FBI, Arab terrorists and suspected terror cells lived in Phoenix, Arizona, as well as in Miami and Hollywood, Florida from December 2000 to April 2001 in direct proximity to the Israeli spy cells."[140]

The Mossad was particularly interested in Mohammed Atta, the terrorist leader, and Marwan al-Shehi, who lived in Hollywood, Florida, cheek-by-jowl with a nest of Israeli agents doing their art student gig, including Hanan Serfati, the ringleader. Serfati rented a series of apartments, one of which was located near the dwelling shared by Atta and Shehi. *Die Zeit* reports that the Mossad was watching the terrorist leader and his chief accomplices *very* closely:

Everything indicates that the terrorists were constantly observed by the Israelis. The chief Israeli agent was staying right near the post office where the terrorists had a mailbox. The Mossad also had its sights on Atta's accomplice Khalid al-Midhar, with whom the CIA was also familiar, but allowed to run free.[141]

But the title of the *Die Zeit* piece—"Next Door to Mohammed Atta"—may be a bit of an overstatement. Schröm writes:

[Mohammed Atta and Marwan al-Shehi] lived in Hamburg before they settled in Hollywood, Florida in order to plan the attacks. A Mossad team was also operating in the same town. The leader, Hanan Serfati, had rented several dwellings. "One of Serfati's apartments was located on the corner of 701st St. and 21st Ave. [sic] in Hollywood, right near the apartment of Atta and al-Shehi," French intelligence reported later.[142]

There is just one problem with this: there is no 701st Street and 21st Avenue in Hollywood, Florida. Serfati's rental was at 701 South 21st Street, about half a mile from Atta's 1818 Jackson Street address. But Serfati rented several apartments in the area, and one could easily have been next door to Mohammed Atta and his confederates, who moved around quite a bit. In addition, the geographical congruity of the Israeli "art students" and the hijacker conspirators was not limited to South Florida, as John Sugg has pointed out.[143]

In any case, *Die Zeit* is quite clear that the Israelis were closely observing Atta and his friends. Yet the Israelis didn't tell us what they were up to until August, 2001: *Der Spiegel* reported that they handed over a list of 19 terrorist suspects, with at least four of the hijackers on it, "a few weeks before" 9/11, but the Americans say that the warning was for attacks "outside the United States."[144]

The warning was non-specific: these were *potential* terrorists. And other discrepancies cloud the picture of Israeli cooperation in this matter. Prior to 9/11, the authorities had detained 140 Israeli in a nationwide round-up, and they rounded up some 60 more after the event. If the Israelis had decided, in August, to come clean with the information they had, then why were federal agents still arresting and detaining our "partners" in the "war on terrorism" in late November and early December?

This was the spin put on this story by *Der Spiegel*:

> Yet soon after, the agents were unmasked by U.S. authorities and deported to Israel. As usual in such cases, the exposure was not made public and only led to disgruntlement between the traditionally competitive intelligence agencies Mossad and CIA. This case proves once again that even in concretely dangerous situations, the U.S. agents were not obliged to cooperate, instead opting to antagonize each other.[145]

This case proves nothing of the sort. What it does prove is 1) that the Israelis had a major spy operation going on in the U.S. in the months prior to 9/11, 2) that the American and Israeli governments lied about it, 3) that the Israelis were not only conducting covert operations against U.S. government facilities but were also hot on the trail of the hijackers, and 4) that some people will go to any lengths to avoid asking some politically explosive questions.

As Mohammed Atta and Marwan al-Shehi prepared for their murderous mission, what were the Mossad agents "next door" doing? Did the "art students" stand behind the terrorists in line at the local supermarket? Did they bump into each other in the street—and how did these dedicated Al Qaeda cadre perceive a group of Israelis living in such close proximity, as foes—or friends? If they were merely watching them, why did the Mossad wait until late August, *after* their spy operation had been discovered to share at least some of this vital information?

Der Spiegel knows better than to implicate the Israelis in anything untoward, and instead mournfully reports that "observation of the...terrorists also ceased" when the "art students" were apprehended. But if the information had been shared then and there—in March, when, according to the task force report, the authorities first became aware of the Mossad's Hollywood-centered South Florida operation—then what prevented the FBI from taking up where the Israelis had left off? *Der Spiegel* is vague about this:

> The Israelis' list with at least four of the 19 assassins from September 11 was apparently not handled by the CIA with the necessary urgency, nor was it forwarded to the FBI. Fact is that the U.S. authorities did not efficiently follow up on the Israeli agents' leads. Information on the Israeli tips has also been made known in the USA during the [Senate intelligence committee 9/11 hearings], which has been ongoing for weeks.[146]

While the FBI is scapegoated for its alleged inefficiency, the Israelis were not exactly forthcoming with their "tips." If it's true, as *Der Spiegel* avers, that the distinguished members of the Senate Committee who investigated 9/11 pinned the blame on their own intelligence agencies, and exonerated the Mossad, one can only wonder why they weren't more critical of the Israelis, who, after all, concealed their activities. Given the technical capabilities of Israeli intelligence in the U.S., and the skills of the agents involved, they knew far more than they are admitting. It is also possible that they were protecting the 9/11 plotters: literally surrounded by Israelis, from San Diego to Texas to South Florida, the hijackers operated in what appears to have been a protective bubble provided by the Mossad. Remember, also, Stability's suggestion that the "art student" gambit was a planned diversion. How long before watching a crime in progress becomes collaboration?

In probing the mystery of how the Mossad and Al Qaeda came to be in such close proximity, I am reminded of this exchange between Brit Hume and Carl Cameron at the end of the December 11 Israeli "art student" broadcast:

> HUME: Carl, what about this question of advanced knowledge of what was going to happen on 9-11? How clear are investigators that some Israeli agents may have known something?

> CAMERON: It's very explosive information, obviously, and there's a great deal of evidence that they say they have collected—none of it necessarily conclusive. It's more when they put it all together. A bigger question, they say, is how could they **not** have known?

The preponderance of evidence makes Israeli foreknowledge of 9/11 a near certainty, and also raises the question of the nature of their complicity: was it merely passive? There is no evidence to indicate otherwise, but the answer has to be: we don't yet know. Perhaps a congressional investigation can uncover the truth. What we do know is this:

1. Elements in U.S. law enforcement are convinced there is an Israeli connection to 9/11, with the thrust of their leaks to the media implying foreknowledge and *passive* collaboration with Bin Laden's *jihad*. As Brit Hume put it in his introduction to Cameron's broadcasts: "Some U.S. investigators believe that there are Israelis again very much engaged in spying in and on the U.S., who may have known things they didn't tell us before September 11."[147]

2. In the winter of 2000, Israel mounted a major covert action in the United States, involving hundreds of Israelis, directed at U.S. government and defense facilities. This activity, which seemed to be a surveillance operation, was monitored and counteracted by federal agents starting in January, with U.S. counterintelligence efforts escalating in the months and weeks prior to 9/11, when at least 140 Israelis were swept up and detained. Most were still being held on 9/11, and 60 more were arrested in the wake of the terrorist attacks.

3. "Urban Moving Systems" was almost certainly a front for Israeli covert operations in the U.S., and its owner has appeared on the FBI's list of terrorist suspects.

4. Israeli spies closely observed the terrorist network that assisted the hijackers between December 2000 and April 2001, and "during their undercover investigations, the Israelis came very close to the later perpetrators of September 11," reports *Der Spiegel*. In Hollywood, Florida, the Israeli spies lived close to Mohammed Atta, where they "observed the seemingly normal flight school students around the clock."

In spite of the denials of "experts" like Cannistrano, these few lines in the *20/20* report stand out: "No one has been able to find a good explanation for why they may have been smiling with the towers of the World Trade Center burning in the background. Both the lawyers for the young men and the Israeli Embassy chalk it up to immature conduct."[148]

Remember, though, what Maria, the eyewitness who observed them through binoculars said: "They were like happy, you know.... They didn't look shocked to me. I thought it was very strange."[149]

Strange, yes, but not inexplicable. Some degree of foreknowledge—and complicity—would explain it. Some knowledge of history would also help to explain it, or at least give us a perspective on the known facts. As the so-called "Lavon

Affair" showed, the Mossad is certainly capable of carrying out a "false flag" operation—to deadly effect.

It was the summer of 1954, and Egypt was witnessing the rise of Colonel Abdul Gamal Nasser, whose brand of Pan-Arabic nationalism put him at the head of a revolution directed against the British military presence in the Suez Canal Zone. Nasser wanted the British out, and the Americans, under President Dwight Eisenhower, were putting pressure on London to leave. The Israelis, for their part, saw the British as a buffer that might protect them against the Arab onslaught, and then-Prime Minister David Ben Gurion did his best to sabotage the withdrawal. When it looked like the British were going along with Eisenhower's wishes, a hardline faction within the Israeli government decided on its own to move. Without the knowledge of Prime Minister Moshe Sharett and Pinhas Lavon, his Defense Minister, Ben Gurion and the head of Israeli intelligence, Colonel Benyamin Givli, ordered the rogue operation that became known by its codename, "Susannah." As the Jewish Agency for Israel explains the internal politics of it:

> Givli was a member of a powerful Defense Ministry clique which often acted independently, or in outright defiance, of the cabinet. They were proteges of Ben Gurion and, although "The Old Man" had left the Premiership for Sde Boker, his Negev desert retreat, a few months before, he was able, through them, to perpetuate the hardline "activist" policies in which he believed.[150]

Colonel Givli's "false flag" operation utilized 11 Egyptian Jews recruited by the Mossad in the early 1950's by Avraham Dar, who had assumed the identity of "John Darling," supposedly a British national native to Gibraltar. According to the Jewish Agency for Israel:

> [Dar] taught the Egyptian Jewish spy ring about underground organizations and conspiratorial tactics. They learned how to make delayed action devices, letter bombs, and the intricacies of photography. In early 1952 most of them came to Israel—secretly, of course—in order to learn sabotage and underground techniques. Most of them fell in love with Israel and vowed to do whatever they could to help.[151]

At the end of their course in terrorist methods, a going away party was organized for the graduates, and it was on this occasion that their mission was dubbed "Operation Susannah," after the fiancée of one of their number, Susan Kauffman. Ms. Kauffman had accompanied the group to Israel and decided to stay.

However, the others, including her betrothed, were to set off for Egypt, where they would await the signal to do their dirty work. They were to listen to Israeli radio, and when the song "Oh! Susannah" was played they would know it was time to act.

Now Givli gave them the signal, and their orders: to plant bombs in crowded public areas such as movie theaters, major railway stations and central post offices in both Alexandria and Cairo, as well as American and British cultural centers, and Egyptian government buildings. Muslim opposition groups would almost certainly be blamed, the Western powers would conclude that Nasser couldn't control the country, and British withdrawal would be delayed if not aborted.

On July 2, 1954, bombs exploded in a few post offices, but the plot didn't get too much farther. The provocateurs had, themselves, been infiltrated: their Israeli handler, Avraham Seidenberg, alias Paul Frank, was a double agent working for Egyptian intelligence.[152]

One of the terrorists, Philip Nathanson, was captured on his way to blow up a movie theater in Alexandria when the bomb in his pocket exploded. As one account has it:

> What was a particularly alarming factor was that outside of the theater a fire engine was waiting, as if expecting them. Philip had the distinct feeling he was being watched. It turned out that he had been. As Philip lay on the ground, he saw startled and frightened faces looking down at him. While somebody shouted "Take care! He may have another bomb!" Philip heard a police sergeant say "Don't worry, don't worry. We were waiting for them. These are the people who set fire to the American library."[153]

That same day, July 14, 1954, Israeli agents, "in clandestine radio contact with Tel Aviv, fire-bombed U.S. Information Service libraries in Cairo and Alexandria." Nathanson's arrest and confession led to more arrests, but the remnants of Israel's cadre of trained terrorists struck again, on July 23, the anniversary of the Egyptian revolution, by setting fires in the Cairo post office, the railway station, and two movie houses.[154]

The rest were rounded up, shortly afterward, and imprisoned: meanwhile, the British-Egyptian rapprochement, under American auspices, had been accomplished. The Ben Gurion-Givli plot had all been for naught. In October, when the Egyptian government announced the discovery of the Israeli spy ring, and put the agents on trial, the Israeli media went into a paroxysm of outrage: to hear them tell it, an anti-Semitic pogrom was in progress, and the whole thing was a frame-up.

There was just one problem: as the trial showed, they were guilty as charged, and the Egyptians, having been in the know from the beginning, had all the evidence. As David Hirst relates in *The Gun and the Olive Branch*:

> This whole episode, which was to poison Israeli political life for a decade and more, came to be known as the "Lavon Affair", for it had been established in the Cairo trial that Lavon, as Minister of Defense, had approved the campaign of sabotage. At least so the available evidence made it appear. But in Israel, Lavon had asked Moshe Sharett for a secret inquiry into a matter about which the cabinet knew nothing. Benyamin Givli, the intelligence chief, claimed that the so-called "security operation" had been authorized by Lavon himself. Two other Bengurion proteges, Moshe Dayan and Shimon Peres, testified against Lavon. Lavon denounced Givli's papers as forgeries and demanded the resignation of all three men. Instead, Sharett ordered Lavon himself to resign and invited Bengurion to come out of retirement and take over the Defense Ministry. It was a triumphant comeback for the "activist" philosophy whose excesses both Sharett and Lavon had tried to modify. It was consummated, a week later, by an unprovoked raid on Gaza, which left thirty-nine Egyptians dead and led to the Suez War of 1956.[155]

Some six years later, however, in the midst of a forgery trial, the truth came to light when a witness testified that he had seen Lavon's forged signature embellishing a document connected to a 1954 "security mishap."[156]

Lavon, whose career had been ruined by his connection to the affair, demanded an investigation, and, despite Ben Gurion's opposition, the truth came out. The investigation showed that "he was a scapegoat pure and simple." On December 25, 1960, the Israeli cabinet unanimously cleared him of all responsibility in the "disastrous security adventure in Egypt."[157]

This was not the last time a rogue intelligence operation would boomerang, with unpleasant consequences for the Jewish state. In 1997, the botched assassination attempt on Khalid Meshal, an official of Hamas, in Amman, Jordan, caused an uproar—and not only in Jordan. A group of Israeli agents, posing as Canadian tourists, sneaked up behind Meshal and tried to inject poison into his ear. But they were overpowered by his bodyguards, and captured: four others involved in the failed attempt sought sanctuary in the Israeli embassy, and Israel was caught with its pants down. In a bizarre turnabout, the Israelis sent a doctor to Jordan with the antidote and saved the life of the man they had tried to murder. That and the release of 70 Hamas prisoners, including the Hamas founder and spiritual leader, Sheikh Yassin, was the price then-Prime Minister Benjamin Netanyahu had to pay to get his agents back. Not the least of which was the polit-

ical price, with a storm in the Knesset over the Mossad's recklessness and amateurish methods, and a controversy as to who should shoulder the responsibility.
As Canadian columnist Eric Margolis reported at the time:

> This is part of a furious battle of leaks raging between Mossad and Netan-
> yahu's cabinet. Some Netanyahu supporters claim the Mossad hit was a rogue
> operation never authorized by the prime minister. Mossad partisans leak back
> that it was all Netanyahu's harebrained idea—and that he's now trying to
> make Mossad chief [Danny] Yatom fall guy for the fiasco. Other critics say a
> hard-line cabal inside Mossad is determined to thwart any peace with Palestin-
> ians—which is likely true.[158]

This hard-line cabal inside Mossad hasn't gone away since the intifada, the rise
of Ariel Sharon and the Reoccupation. If anything, its influence has
increased—along with its boldness. The willingness of rogue elements within the
Mossad to pursue their own agenda is, as we have seen, a consistent factor in the
history of the Israeli intelligence community—that and a penchant for criminal-
ity not limited to targeted assassinations, but extending to terror as a method to
achieve foreign policy goals.

Clearly, what took place in the period leading up to 9/11 was not the equivalent of the Lavon Affair: no one is saying that the Mossad carried out terrorist
actions in the United States, or that they hijacked those planes and rammed them
into the World Trade Center and the Pentagon. The contention coming from
elements within U.S. law enforcement agencies, and expressed through leaks to
the media, is that the Israelis knew about Al Qaeda's plans—or at least their
intentions—and watched as they prepared the ground for 9/11.

While the Israeli "art student" cells that roiled the intelligence waters in the
crucial days prior to 9/11 did not engage in terrorism, certainly their activities
around U.S. government facilities at that time were invasive, and properly classified as hostile. If the Dominik Suter-Urban Mover-Mossad connection can be
pursued all the way to the end—that is, all the way to extraditing Suter to the
U.S.—it would at the very least explain why the U.S. government put a known
Israeli agent's name on the same suspect list as Mohammed Atta and Hani Han-
jour. It could establish some degree of Israeli foreknowledge—and, in effect,
complicity.

If it is true that the Israelis knew and didn't tell us, then the question of
motive becomes paramount. Why would the Israelis hold on so tightly to information, the disclosure of which might have prevented 9/11?

One can explain this failure of the "special relationship" between the U.S. and Israel as a simple desire on the part of the Mossad to protect its sources and methods. This, after all, is the prime directive of any and all intelligence agencies: such secrets are jealously guarded, and stealing them is the equivalent of making off with the crown jewels. Which is why the betrayal of Jonathan Pollard was such a blow to the U.S.

The documents Pollard provided to Israel were valuable precisely because they were raw data that revealed vital sources of information. Learning the methods by which American intelligence collected data and to whom it was distributed gave the Mossad insights into our military infrastructure and capabilities, as well as invaluable specific information, i.e. the identities of agents and the location of facilities. According to Seymour Hersh, American intelligence officials believe much of what he stole and passed on to the Israelis wound up in Soviet hands, leading to a spate of executions of American agents.[159]

The extreme sensitivity of this information accounted for the absolute refusal of the U.S. military and intelligence community to countenance any talk of Pollard's release, even though his supporters in the U.S., as well as successive Israeli governments, have never stopped asking for clemency. On the face of it, it's a difficult case to make: here is a thief who made off with the crown jewels, and unloaded them for a paltry sum—it's a tough row to hoe, but not completely barren. One could indeed make the argument that Pollard was helping an ally, while disputing the damage done, and make it sound convincing. But what about clemency for an alleged ally who watched the 9/11 plot unfold from a safe distance—and did nothing to stop it?

History repeats itself, but never exactly. The Lavon Affair was indeed a tragedy, albeit a farcical one—especially for the Egyptian Jews left to rot in prison by the Israelis, who didn't officially acknowledge the operation until much later. It was tragic, also, for the Egyptian Jewish community, which was cast in the role of a fifth column for Israel, even though most of them wanted nothing to do with Zionism and the Israeli government. As Hirst reminds us:

> The welfare of Oriental Jewry in their various homelands was, as we have seen, Israel's last concern. And in July 1954 it had other worries. It was feeling isolated and insecure. Its Western friends—let alone the rest of the world—were unhappy about its aggressive behavior. The U.S. Assistant Secretary of State advised it to "drop the attitude of the conqueror."[160]

Nothing much seems to have changed over the years. At the end of 2002, the Lavon Affair was reenacted when it was discovered that the Mossad had tried to recruit Palestinians into a phony Al Qaeda cell in Gaza.[161] The operation was uncovered when PLO security traced cell-phone calls and emails to potential recruits back to Israel, as well as Germany and Lebanon.[162]

The sheer boldness of their recruitment methods, such as this message to would-be members cited by ABC News, is what may have given them away:

> After receiving reports from your brothers in the area about your good morals and Islamic beliefs … we appeal to you to work within the ranks of the *mujahideen* (Muslim fighters) and we will support you with money and weapons. Call us at this number … and identify yourself as Abu Anas. The telephone call should be made between three and five in the afternoon…After you read the letter and understand its content, burn it.
>
> (Signed), Your brother and humble slave of God, Osama bin Laden.[163]

Recruits to this faux-Al Qaeda were given weapons (most of them didn't work) and money provided by "Palestinian collaborators with Israel,"[164] three of whom are in a Palestinian jail. According to PLO "preventive security" chief Rashid Abu Shbak, some of the money "was transferred from bank accounts in Jerusalem or Israel."

These revelations came in the wake of Israeli Prime Minister Ariel Sharon's claim that Al Qaeda is behind recent attacks on Israel, and is present in the occupied territories and Lebanon. A phony "Al Qaeda" website has been set up, which we are supposed to believe is the voice of Bin Laden in cyberspace: its recent pronouncement that a Palestinian "branch" of Al Qaeda has been formed was duly reported by the *Washington Post*, which also transcribed the lamentation of one Rachel Bronson, director of Middle East Studies at the Council on Foreign Relations: "'The idea that al Qaeda is establishing a special cell to focus on Israelis is horrifying news…'…Al Qaeda's role could be extremely destabilizing, she added, because 'it will be weighing in on the side of Hamas,' the Palestinian Islamic group that launches suicide bombings against Israeli civilians and has been deemed a terrorist organization by the U.S. government."[165]

What is horrifying is that Israel is now in the business of impersonating Al Qaeda. Israel's great achievement in the political and diplomatic realm has been to draw the unleashed anger of the American giant away from the perpetrators of 9/11 and toward its own enemies: Saddam Hussein, Hamas, and the fictitious "Islamic Al-Qaeda of Palestine," which exists only "by way of deception," to borrow a phrase from the official motto of the Mossad.

"By way of deception, thou shalt do war" is a principle the Israeli government has always lived up to. Juxtaposed against the mounting evidence of an Israeli connection to 9/11, the exposure of the Mossad's latest "false flag" operation raises the possibility that they have done the same elsewhere, perhaps in the U.S. If the Israelis are running phony "Al Qaeda" cells in Palestine and Lebanon, they are perfectly capable of the same behavior in South Florida, or New York.

Nothing much seems to have changed over the years. Intransigent Israel is still besieged by terrorism at home, and the rising tide of public opinion abroad. It is still being chastised by the U.S. State Department, and subjected to constant pressure by its primary ally and patron to compromise what it regards as vital national security interests. It still finds itself isolated and insecure, unsure of its Western friends, if not downright paranoid. The stage is set, then, for a Ben Gurion, a Colonel Givli, a man of action, and we have a variation, not a repeat of history, in which the Marxian aphorism has been reversed, and farce has been transmuted into towering tragedy.

5

The Collaborators

Having established the factual basis of the Israeli connection to 9/11—if not the precise extent of Israeli foreknowledge—it is instructive to raise the question of motivation, and ask: who benefits?

Look at the position of Israel vis-à-vis the United States prior to 9/11, and compare it to the post-9/11 era. The Israelis went from being a troublesome ally whose rocky relations with Washington increasingly teetered on the edge of outright confrontation, to our one and only reliable ally in the region, for whose sake the U.S. decided to launch a war against Iraq—a war that promises to spread throughout the region, pitting the U.S. and Israel against the Arab regimes.

On the possibility of an American attack on Iraq, Professor Paul W. Schroeder, of the University of Illinois at Urbana-Champaign, wrote:

> It would represent something to my knowledge unique in history. It is common for great powers to try to fight wars by proxy, getting smaller powers to fight for their interests. This would be the first instance I know where a great power (in fact, a superpower) would do the fighting as the proxy of a small client state.[166]

The possibility that Saddam Hussein might develop or acquire "weapons of mass destruction" acted as a deterrent to Israel's ambitions in the region. Iraq was attacked, conquered, and occupied because Saddam was a danger to Tel Aviv, not Hoboken, New Jersey. Anyone who believes the ongoing Iraq war is not being fought for Israel's sake needs a lesson in elementary geography. In a classic case of form following function, Iraq today is merely the American version of Israel's occupied territories in the West Bank and Gaza.

9/11 in and of itself did not propel us into the Israelis' tight embrace: an entire propaganda and agitational apparatus, the above-ground and out-front version of the Israeli "art students" operation, had its work cut out for it, and performed admirably. The machinery was there, ready to be activated at the right moment, and no sooner had the smoke clouding the New York City skyline partially cleared then the War Party was pressing its program of a civilizational conflict between Islam and the West—a war pitting the U.S., Israel, and what few allies they could garner against the entire Muslim world.

In less than a year, the War Party managed to divert the anger of the American people from Osama bin Laden to Saddam Hussein—Israel's principal enemy in the Middle East. And Israel's amen corner in the U.S. asserted itself as never before. America's Likudniks rallied to the sound of the war drums, and kept up an incessant chorus of cries for an immediate attack on Iraq. Furthermore, these same forces also launched a preemptive strike against the nascent antiwar movement, charging war opponents with being objectively "anti-Semitic," as the neo-conservative Andrew Sullivan argued:

> America's anti-war movement, still puny and struggling is showing signs of being hijacked by one of the oldest and darkest prejudices there is. Perhaps it was inevitable. The conflict against Islamo-fascism obviously circles back to the question of Israel. Fanatical anti-semitism, as bad or even worse than Hitler's, is now a cultural norm across much of the Middle East. It's the acrid glue that unites Saddam, Arafat, Al-Qaeda, Hezbollah, Iran and the Saudis. And if you campaign against a war against that axis, you're bound to attract people who share these prejudices.[167]

A smear campaign was launched against the anti-war movement because its advocates dared to state the obvious: that the national interests of the U.S. and Israel are not identical. The great achievement of Israel's powerful lobby is that it has succeeded in erasing the line that separates the two. We know that Israel has cracked American communications systems, spied on U.S. law enforcement agencies, and commands an underground army in the U.S. to do its bidding. Their above-ground army is no less efficient.

Christian fundamentalists, who call themselves "Christian Zionists," and wield enormous influence in the Republican party, and more traditional Zionist groups, historically associated with the Democrats, have combined in an unholy alliance united around a single issue: unconditional support to the policies of Israel's Likud government. In Congress, in the media, and on the streets they are mobilizing behind Sharon's foreign policy just as effectively as the old Communist Party of the Popular Front period rallied around Stalin's. Indeed, the comparison to the Popular Front—when the Communists were in an alliance with New Deal Democrats—is an almost precise analogy. A world war, a common enemy, a censorious attitude toward any and all dissent: all the familiar elements are there, including top administration officials clearly sympathetic to the cause of a foreign ally.

In this context, to present the evidence for Israeli foreknowledge of 9/11 is to invite all sorts of trouble, not the least of which is the accusation of anti-Semitism. But the policies of the Sharon government are no more representative of Jewish opinion worldwide than the rantings of Robert Mugabe are globally emblematic of blacks. The redefinition of anti-Semitism to mean anyone and everyone who criticizes Israel is a double-edged sword. For the promiscuous use of this loaded term by Sullivan and others devalues its meaning—and allows real anti-Semites an opening.

The systematic cover-up by the U.S. government of the Israeli spy ring, and its connection to 9/11, is hardly inexplicable. It stands to reason that our hapless law enforcement agencies, outmaneuvered by Al Qaeda and the Israelis, would want to keep the history of their monumental incompetence a secret. But at some point incompetence turns into complicity.

Revealing Israel's role in 9/11 would have led to all sorts of embarrassing questions, starting with: how is it that the Israelis were in a position to launch a covert action, on U.S. territory, on the scale of their pre-9/11 activities, involving hundreds of agents? How did they gain access to sensitive communications networks? How did they get so physically close to the hijackers—at the same time the bureaucrats at FBI headquarters were busy obstructing their agency's own investigation into the hijacking plot?

In the wake of 9/11, federal law enforcement agencies have been seen in a new—and especially cruel—light. Where were they when Osama bin Laden's ghouls were plotting the destruction of the WTC and the Pentagon on our own soil? The picture that has emerged, at least up until very recently, is one of incompetence on the level of the Keystone Kops, a tragi-comedy of errors—but, with further analysis, it appears that something more sinister than stupidity, bureaucratic ineptitude, and inter-departmental competition has been at work. For nothing less than treason is the reason yet another FBI whistle-blower made headlines with revelations that make veteran FBI agent Coleen Rowley's charges of high-level obstructionism in the Zacarias Moussaoui case look relatively innocuous. "2 FBI Whistle-Blowers Allege Lax Security, Possible Espionage," the *Washington Post* headline modestly averred.[168]

Sibel Edmonds, 32, a former wiretap translator in the FBI's Washington field office, stepped forward with a stunning narrative of official obstructionism and high-level espionage that breaks down into four stunning accusations:

1. One of her fellow FBI translators, later identified in court documents as Jan Dickerson,[169] "belonged to the Middle Eastern organization whose taped conversations she had been translating for FBI counterintelligence agents," according to the *Post*. "'This person told us she worked for our target organization,'" Edmonds says. "These are the people we are targeting, monitoring." Dickerson also met with "a foreign official subject to the surveillance." Furthermore, says Edmonds, Dickerson (and her husband, U.S. Air Force Maj. Douglas Dickerson) "tried to recruit her to join the targeted foreign group."

2. As Edmonds wrote in a March letter to the inspector general's office: "Investigations are being compromised. Incorrect or misleading translations are being sent to agents in the field. Translations are being blocked and circumvented."

3. This mysterious "Middle Eastern organization" had a definite preference insofar as how the FBI's wiretaps were translated—and by whom. Edmonds says that Dickerson presented her with "a list dividing up individuals whose phone lines were being secretly tapped: Under the plan, Dickerson would translate conversations of her former co-workers in the target organization, and Edmonds would handle other phone calls." When Edmonds refused, Dickerson "told her that her lack of cooperation could put her family in danger."

4. When she went to her bosses with this information, Edmonds—instead of being thanked, and given a medal—was summarily fired for being "disruptive."

One has to ask: "disruptive" of what? The spy nest ensconced so firmly in the upper reaches of US "law enforcement"? In her lawsuit against the U.S. government, Edmonds claims that Dickerson "blocked the translation of intercepted conversation involv[ing] several Turkish acquaintances of Dickerson's who were the subject of FBI investigations."[170] CBS News reports:

> Edmonds also says that when she reviewed Dickerson's translations of those tapes, she found that Dickerson had left out information crucial to the FBI's investigation, information that Edmonds says would have revealed that the Turkish intelligence officer had spies working for him inside the U.S. State Department and at the Pentagon.[171]

The diplomatic, military, and intelligence links between Turkey and Israel are well-established. As journalist Eric Margolis points out: "Turkey is assuming command of the western 'protective' force in Kabul, Afghanistan, propping up the US-installed regime of Hamid Karzai. Turkish intelligence works closely with CIA and Israel's Mossad against Islamic militants. Turkey has become a close ally and major arms customer of Israel."[172] Author Gordon Thomas agrees. "For Israel," Gordon writes, "a close working relationship with Turkey is an important element in its strategic and diplomatic survival in the region." He points out that, without the help of the Israeli intelligence agency, Ankara would never have gotten its hands on Abdullah Ocalan, the Kurdish rebel leader: "It would be a 'black operation'—meaning that Mossad's own involvement would never surface publicly. If successful, all the credit would go to Turkish intelligence. Mossad would operate on a strictly need-to-know basis as far as that service went."[173]

In the case of the Edmonds-Dickerson caper, all the "credit" is once again going to the Turks. In any case, whomever was behind this penetration of a key U.S. intelligence agency was certainly aggressively pursuing a strategy of obstruction. Edmonds says that Dickerson, accompanied by her husband, rushed over to Edmonds' home one Sunday and suggested that Edmonds "join the group." The *Post* reports the following recap of their conversation:

> He said, "Are you a member of the particular organization?" [He said,] "It's a very good place to be a member. There are a lot of advantages of being with this organization and doing things together"—this is our targeted organization—"and one of the greatest things about it is you can have an early, an unexpected, early retirement. And you will be totally set if you go to that specific country."[174]

What is shocking, however, is the direct connection of this treason to the misdirection of American anti-terrorist efforts. The *Post* reports:

> The FBI confirmed that Edmonds's coworker had been part of an organization that was a target of top-secret surveillance and that the same coworker had "unreported contacts" with a foreign government official subject to the surveillance, according to a letter from the two senators to the Justice Department's Office of the Inspector General. In addition, the linguist failed to translate two communications from the targeted foreign government official, the letter said."[175]

Edmonds' own bosses didn't want to hear it: instead of investigating, they fired her. So Edmonds went to Senators Chuck Grassley and Patrick J. Leahy, both of whom are demanding answers. "This whistleblower raised serious questions about potential security problems and the integrity of important translations made by the FBI," Grassley said in a statement. "She made these allegations in good faith and even though the deck was stacked against her. The FBI even admits to a number of her allegations, and on other allegations, the bureau's explanation leaves me skeptical."[176]

Leaving aside for the moment the question of why, in the post-9/11 era, a patriotic American with vital information on spies in our law enforcement apparatus would have the deck "stacked against her," as Senator Grassley puts it, there is the matter of the translation "glitch" attributed to the National Security Agency. According to the *Washington Post*, this left two key Arabic-language messages intercepted "on the eve of the Sept. attacks"—"The match is about to begin" and "Tomorrow is zero hour"—untranslated until Sept. 12.[177]

The explanation given is that the sources weren't top priority—i.e. they didn't involve Osama bin Laden and his top circle—but were important enough to account for the relatively short two-day lapse. The blame is being placed on lack of resources, human fallibility, anything but a deliberate policy of sabotage—in spite of Ms. Edmonds' clear testimony of foreign interference in the NSA's vital translation section.

Not since Whittaker Chambers exposed a Stalinist nest high in the topmost branches of the U.S. government has the light been shone on such a deep—and dangerous—penetration of the nation's high-security innards. How many more 9/11's do we have to witness before Americans see through the scare tactics, the cover-ups, and reluctance of the media and political elites to ask the hard questions?

In her sensational and widely covered testimony before Congress, veteran FBI agent Coleen Rowley declined to use the term "cover-up" to characterize the FBI's official statements since Sept. 11. Instead, she averred, she would "carefully" describe it as follows: "I feel that certain facts, including the following, have, up to now, been omitted, downplayed, glossed over and/or mis-characterized in an effort to avoid or minimize personal and/or institutional embarrassment on the part of the FBI and/or perhaps even for improper political reasons."

In her now-famous memo, Rowley related that, around the Minnesota FBI office where she was working frantically to trace the terrorist trail: "Almost everyone's first question was: 'Why? Why would an FBI agent(s) deliberately sabotage a case?'...Jokes were actually made that the key FBIHQ personnel had to be spies or moles, like Robert Hansen [actually Hanssen], who were actually working for Osama bin Laden."

Ms. Edmonds is suing the U.S. government, and her lawyers make a few tren-
chant points. After pointing out that their client's disclosures were not properly
investigated, they write:

> She was instructed by high level FBI management not to purse any com-
> plaints, and threatened with retaliation if she continued to report wrongdo-
> ing....The front-line of the war on terrorism has been directly undermined by
> the FBI's failures to act on our client's reports. The FBI failed to promptly
> correct these problems and instead waged war against its own whistleblower.
> This is unforgivable in the post-9/11 world.[178]

What is truly unforgivable is the government's response: stonewalling. The
director of public affairs for the U.S. Department of Justice, Barbara Comstock—the same government spokesperson who characterized the Israeli "art student" spy story as an "urban myth"—tersely announced:

> To prevent disclosure of certain classified and sensitive national security infor-
> mation, Attorney General Ashcroft today asserted the state secrets privilege in
> Sibel Edmonds v. Department of Justice.....The Department of Justice also
> filed a motion to dismiss the case, because the litigation creates substantial
> risks of disclosing classified and sensitive national security information that
> could cause serious damage to our country's security.[179]

The Edmonds affair, it is safe to say, shows that the security of U.S. law
enforcement is seriously compromised—quite possibly at the highest levels.

The sheer scope of Israel's pre-9/11 operation on American soil required the
collaboration of U.S. government officials, at least in a passive sense. They not
only looked the other way when it came to Israeli covert actions in the U.S., but
also continued to lie about it even after the story had come out. And they are still
lying about it.

The cover-up is important. For the real story of the prelude to 9/11 would put
that event into a whole new perspective. Its wide dissemination and acceptance
would smash the "civilizational" war paradigm that neoconservatives hold up as
the lesson of 9/11. If Israeli intelligence withheld vital information from U.S.
authorities, if they stood by and watched as 19 madmen dreamed of an endless
supply of virgins in Paradise, then why is America still championing the Israeli
cause? This is a question that will doubtless occur to many Americans, as evidence of Israel's treacherous role in this whole bungled affair becomes more
widely known.

The most outrageous aspect of the Israeli incursion is the excruciatingly slow rate at which the facts leaked out—without much help from the mainstream media. The *Washington Post* reported only the most perfunctory version, and then nearly always framed by official denials. The *New York Times*—the "newspaper of record"—has yet to report the story. However, the story survived and developed, making periodic appearances in large-circulation venues, and then dropping out of sight altogether. Americans following up on Carl Cameron's pioneering report for Fox News had to read the overseas media: *Le Monde*, the British papers, *Ha'aretz, Die Zeit, Der Spiegel*, and "alternative" sources such as Antiwar.com.

American and British papers made much of news reports about purported Saudi financial aid to the hijackers, in spite of the tenuous nature of the alleged connection: the money passed from the bank account of the Saudi ambassador's wife to the friend of a friend of a friend who loaned the money to someone else, who then aided some of the hijackers.[180] On the other hand, only *Ha'aretz*, an Israeli daily newspaper, carried the news that accounts in Israeli banks had been used to fund terrorist activities.[181]

The Bank of Israel "has obtained information that several accounts held in Israeli banks may have been used to fund terrorist activities." According to the Bank, however, the Banking Secrecy Law forbids them from turning the information over to the Justice Ministry—or, presumably, American law enforcement agencies.

In the wake of 9/11, all Israeli accounts were checked against a list of suspected terrorists circulated by the American authorities. According to *Ha'aretz*: "Several suspicious accounts and financial transactions were found. The Bank of Israel has confirmed the existence of accounts believed to have been connected to the financing of terrorist operations but refused to state how many suspect accounts had been uncovered and to which terrorist organizations they were connected."[182]

Evidence of foreign involvement—and a massive cover-up—continues to accumulate. In an interview with Gwen Ifill of the PBS "News Hour," Senator Bob Graham (D-Florida) was asked about the recently completed Senate committee report analyzing the intelligence failures that preceded the 9/11 terror attack: "Are there elements in this report, which are classified that Americans should know about but can't?" The Senator's reply should have garnered mile-high headlines:

Yes, going back to your question about what was the greatest surprise. I agree with what Senator Shelby said the degree to which agencies were not communicating was certainly a surprise but also I was surprised at the evidence that there were foreign governments involved in facilitating the activities of at least some of the terrorists in the United States.[183]

According to Graham, who also points to the Saudis, more than one foreign government was likely involved in 9/11. And the danger has not passed:

I am stunned that we have not done a better job of pursuing that to determine if other terrorists received similar support," he said, "and, even more important, if the infrastructure of a foreign government assisting terrorists still exists for the current generation of terrorists who are here planning the next plots. To me that is an extremely significant issue and most of that information is classified, I think overly-classified."[184]

"Evidence linking these Israelis to 9-11 is classified." That is what Carl Cameron was told when he asked a highly placed government investigator for details about the Israeli connection to 9/11: "I cannot tell you about evidence that has been gathered. It's classified information."

"I believe the American people should know the extent of the challenge that we face in terms of foreign government involvement," Senator Graham continued. "That would motivate the government to take action."

"Are you suggesting that you are convinced that there was a state sponsor behind 9/11?" asked PBS news anchor Gwen Ifill.

Graham answered: "I think there is very compelling evidence that at least some of the terrorists were assisted not just in financing—although that was part of it—by a sovereign foreign government and that we have been derelict in our duty to track that down, make the further case, or find the evidence that would indicate that that is not true and we can look for other reasons why the terrorists were able to function so effectively in the United States."

Ifill then asked: "Do you think that will ever become public, which countries you're talking about?"

"It will become public," answered Graham, "at some point when it's turned over to the archives, but that's 20 or 30 years from now. And, we need to have this information now because it's relevant to the threat that the people of the United States are facing today."[185]

This burgeoning scandal underscores why the two-sided Manichean view promoted by George W. Bush in his "war on terrorism" is fundamentally false.

"You're either with us," he intoned, "or against us." But what about the Israelis? When they were shadowing the hijackers and learning their secrets, were they with us—or against us? When they were descending on government offices and military facilities, in what Stability characterized as a diversionary tactic,[186] were they with us—or against us? When they issued a vague warning far too late, when they certainly knew far more than they were telling—were they with us, or against us?

We cannot wait twenty or thirty years to find out. The idea that Americans must remain in the dark about 9/11 until their government decides to let them see what is in the archives is an insult to the memory of those who died, contrary to the concept of a government that is answerable to the people—and a danger to us all.

Endnotes

1. George W. Bush, "Address to a Joint Session of Congress," September 20, 2001;
   http://www.whitehouse.gov/news/releases/2001/09/20010920-8.html.

2. U.S. authorities have recently uncovered a suspected twentieth hijacker: see Toni Locy, "FBI has new 9/11 hijacking suspect Operative left USA before plan realized," *USA Today*, November 5, 2003;
   http://www.usatoday.com/usatonline/20031105/5651228s.htm.

3. "9/11 Bombshe ll: Bush Knew," *New York Post*, May 16, 2002.

4. Andrew Gumbel and Jason Bennetto, "Bush was given hijack warning by British intelligence,' [UK] *Independent*, May 18, 2002.

5. James Ridgeway, "U.S. Ignored Warnings From French," *Village Voice*, May 28th, 2002.

6. *Frankfurter Allegemeine Zeitung*, September 14, 2001

7. Putin interview with MSNBC, September 15, 2002.

8. "Argentinians Say They Heard Terror Alert Weeks Before 9/11," *The Forward*, May 31, 2002.

9. Douglas Davis, "Mossad warned CIA of attacks," *Jerusalem Post*, September 17, 2001.

10. Joe Panossian, "Egypt Leader Says he Warned Armerica," Associated Press, December 7, 2001.

11. John K. Cooley, "Other unheeded warnings before 9/11?," *Christian Science Monitor*, May 23, 2002.

12. http://www.ncix.gov/news/2001/mar01.html.

13. At least sixty were detained after 9/11/01: see John Mintz, "60 Israelis on Tourist Visas Detained Since Sept. 11," *Washington Post*, November 23, 2001. Salon.com reported: "According to one account, some 140 Israeli nationals were detained or arrested between March 2001 and Sept. 11,

2001." See Christopher Ketcham, "The Israeli 'Art Student' Mystery," Salon, May 7, 2002; http://www.salon.com/news/feature/2002/05/07/students/index_np.html.

14. http://www.ncix.gov/news/2001/mar01.html.

15. "Suspicious Activities Involving Israeli Art Students," no date [summer, 2001], http://cryptome.org/dea-il-spy.htm.

16. Ibid.

17. Ibid..

18. Anna Werner, "The Defenders," KHOU-TV, October 1, 2002; cited in Christopher Ketcham, "The Israeli 'Art Student' Mystery," May 7,2002; http://www.salon.com/news/feature/2002/05/07/students/index_np.html.

19. Paulo Lima, "Five Men Detained as Suspected Conspirators," Bergen, N.J., Record, September 12, 2002.

20. Ibid.

21. Yuval Dror, "Odigo says workers were warned of attack," Ha'aretz, November 27, 2001; http://www.haaretzdaily.com/hasen/pages/ShArt.jhtml?itemNo=77744&contrassID=/has%5C.

22. John Mintz, "60 Israelis on Tourist Visas Detained Since Sept. 11," Washington Post, November 23, 2001; http://www.washingtonpost.com/ac2/wp-dyn?pagename=article&node=&contentId=A3879-2001Nov22&notFound=true.

23. Jane's Intelligence Digest, March 13, 2002.

24. Martin Peretz, "Israel, the United States, and Evil," The New Republic, September 24, 2001; http://www.tnr.com/092401/peretz092401.html.

25. Although a story about the viewers' response to the Cameron series remains on the Fox News website, the story itself was pulled less than a week after it was posted, and has yet to reappear. See http://www.foxnews.com/story/0,2933,40706,00.html and http://www.foxnews.com/story/0,2933,40679,00.html. A facsimile of Part I can be found here: http://www.mafhoum.com/press2/75P81.htm. The full text—hereinafter Cameron, Fox News—can be found here: http://www.intellex.com/~rigs/page1/wtc/spies.htm.

26. Ibid.

27. Ibid.

28. Ibid.

29. "Suspicious Activities Involving Israeli Art Students at DEA Facilities," http://cryptome.org/dea-il-spy.htm.

30. Sylvain Cypel, "An Enigma: Vast Israeli Spy Network Dismantled in the U.S.," *Le Monde*, March 5, 2002; http://www.antiwar.com/rep/lemonde1.html.

31. Cameron, Fox News.

32. Ibid.

33. J, Michael Waller and Paul M. Rodriguez, "FBI Probes Espionage at Clinton White House," *Insight*, May 29, 2000. Reposted December 19, 2001, http://www.insightmag.com/main.cfm/include/detail/storyid/160595.html.

34. Cited in ibid.

35. Ibid.

36. Cameron, Fox News.

37. Ibid.

38. Ibid.

39. Ibid.

40. Ibid.

41. See the introductory comments prefacing the body of the report.

42. See Evan Thomas, "The Castro Plot Thickens—Again," *Washington Post*, June 28, 1998; see also the *Church Committee Report, Final Summary*, 94th Congress, 2d Session Senate Report No. 94-755, U.S. Government Printing Office, 1976; http://vander.hashish.com/articles/misc/churchfinal.html.

43. See Chalmers Johnson, *Blowback: The Costs and Consequences of American Empire*, Henry Holt, 2000.

44. William Safire, "Inside the Bunker," *New York Times*, September 13, 2001.

45. Ibid.

46. "Ashcroft: Critics of new terror measures undermine effort," CNN, December 7, 2001; http://www.cnn.com/2001/U.S./12/06/inv.ashcroft.hearing/.

47. Gershom Gorenberg, "A Foreigner in Solitary in America," *Washington Post*, December 7, 2001; http://www.washingtonpost.com/ac2/wp-dyn?pagename=article&node=&contentId=A11458-2001Dec7&notFound=true.

48. Ibid.

49. Ibid.

50. Ibid.

51. Melissa Radler, "Israel dismisses report it didn't share WTC attack data," *Jerusalem Post*, December 20, 2001; http://www.jpost.com/Editions/2001/12/20/News/News.40286.html.

52. Howard Kurtz, "The Reluctant Scrutiny of 9/11," *Washington Post*, February 7, 2002; http://www.washingtonpost.com/ac2/wp-dyn?pagename=article&node=&contentId=A38059-2002Feb7.

53. Citied in ibid.

54. Ibid.

55. Ibid.

56. Ibid.

57. "Bush asks Daschle to limit Sept. 11 probes," CNN, January 29, 2002; http://www.cnn.com/2002/ALLPOLITICS/01/29/inv.terror.probe/index.html.

58. Kurtz, "Reluctant Scrutiny."

59. Cited in Mohamed Hakki, "What Tiger?", *El Ahram*, January 24, 2002; http://www.ahram.org.eg/weekly/2002/570/in1.htm.

60. Sylvain Cypel, An Enigma: Vast Israeli Spy Network Dismantled in the U.S.," *Le Monde*, March 5, 2002; http://www.antiwar.com/rep/lemonde1.html.

61. *Intelligence Online*, March 14, 2002.

62. Ibid.

63. http://www.intelligenceonline.com/images/newversion/reseau/HTML/ isr-net_A.htm.

64. Sylvain Cypel, "An Enigma…".

65. John Mintz and Dan Eggen, "Reports of Israeli Spy Ring Dismissed," *Washington Post*, March 6, 2002; http://www.washingtonpost.com/ac2/ wp-dyn?pagename=article&node=&contentId=A45802-2002Mar6& notFound=true.

66. Agence France Press, "French Website Threatens to Publish Israeli Spy Ring Report," March 5, 2002.

67. Jeff Shields, "Israeli art students suspected of spying," South Florida *Sun-Sentinel*, March 7, 2002.

68. Daniel Pipes, "An Israeli spy network in the United States?", *New York Post*, March 11, 2002.

69. Ibid.

70. http://www.ncix.gov/news/2001/mar01.html#a1.

71. Sylvain Cypel, "An Enigma"; Cameron, Fox News.

72. "A majority of those questioned has [sic] stated they served in military intelligence, electronic signal intercept, or explosive ordinance units." "Suspicious Activities Involving Israeli Art Students at DEA Facilities," http://cryptome.org/dea-il-spy.htm.

73. Cameron, Fox News.

74. *Intelligence Online*, March 14, 2002. See also Sylvain Cypel, "An Enigma."

75. Paul M. Rodriguez, "Intelligence Agents or Art Students?", *Insight*, March 11, 2002; http://www.insightmag.com/main.cfm/include/detail/storyid/ 207226.html.

76. Connie Cass, "'Suspicious' Art Students Deported by U.S.," Associated Press, March 10, 2002.

77. Rodriguez, "Intelligence Agents or Art Students?"

78. "NJ Locations Searched In Connection With Terror Attacks, Airport Shut Down Again," WABC-TV, New York, September 14, 2001; http://abclocal.go.com/wabc/news/WABC_091401_airports.html.

79. Adam Lisberg, "Five hijack suspects had links to N.J.," Bergen County *Record*, November 15, 2001.

80. "The 700 Club," September 13, 2001, transcript at: http://www.pfaw.org/issues/right/robertson_falwell.html.

81. April 15, 2002; http://www.defenselink.mil/speeches/2002/s20020415-depsecdef.html.

82. Rodriguez, "Intelligence Agents or Art Students?"

83. Ibid.

84. Ibid.

85. James Taranto, "Best of the Web Today," *Wall Street Journal*, March 11, 2002; http://www.opinionjournal.com/best/?id=105001752.

86. Ibid.

87. *Washington Post*, March 9, 2002.

88. Rick Hellman, "Caught in a Crackdown," Kansas City *Jewish Chronicle*, n.d.; http://www.jewsweek.com/society/171.htm.

89. Anna Werner, "The Defenders," KHOU-TV, Houston, Texas, October 1, 2001.

90. Pipes, "An Israeli spy network in the United States?"

91. Marc Perelman, "Spy Rumors Fly on Gusts of Truth," *The Forward*, March 15, 2002; http://www.forward.com/issues/2002/02.03.15/news2.html.

92. Ibid.

93. Ibid.

94. Tallie Lieberman, "Israeli cable companies decide not to renew contracts with CNN," Associated Press, August 2, 2002.

95. Jean-Charles Brisard and Guillaume Dasquie, *Forbidden Truth: U.S.-Taliban Secret Oil Diplomacy and the Failed Hunt for Bin Laden*, Thunder's Mouth Press/Nation Books, New York, 2002.

96. Justin Raimondo, "Israel and 9/11," November 28, 2001; http://www.antiwar.com/justin/j112801.html.

97. Perelman, "Spy Rumors Fly on Gusts of Truth."

98. James Bone and Ross Dunn, "Security Council endorses two-state vision," [UK] *Times*, March 14, 2002.

99. Marc Perelman, "FBI Probe Defuses Israeli Spying Rumors," *The Forward*, March 15, 2002; http://www.forward.com/issues/2002/02.03.15/news6.html.

100. http://www.movingadvocateteam.com/.

101. Dan Benson, "Movers' boss claims anti-Semitism," Milwaukee *Journal-Sentinel*, May 1, 2002; http://www.jsonline.com/news/ozwash/apr02/39684.asp

102. http://cryptome.org/dea-il-spy.htm.

103. Ibid.

104. Ibid.

105. John Sugg, "The spies who came in from the art sale," *Weekly Planet*, March 30, 2002; http://www.atlanta.creativeloafing.com/2002-03-20/fishwrapper.html.

106. Juliet Eilperin, "Democrat Implies Sept. 11 Administration Plot," *Washington Post*, April 12, 2002; http://www.washingtonpost.com/ac2/wp-dyn?pagename=article&node=&contentId=A34565-2002Apr11.

107. "Allies and Espionage," *Jane's Intelligence Digest*, March 14, 2002; http://www.janes.com/security/international_security/news/jid/jid020313_1_n.shtml.

108. Christopher Ketcham, "The Israeli 'art student' mystery," Salon.com, May 7, 2002; http://real-info.1accesshost.com/artstudents.html

109. http://www.verisign.com/corporate/news/2002/pr_20020603a.html.

110. Ibid.

111. Paul Wouters and Patrick Smits, "Nederlandse tapkamers niet kosjer," *C'T*, December 19, 2002; http://www.fnl.nl/ct-nl/archief2002/ct2002-12/aftappen.htm.

112. Ibid.

113. Cited in Rodriguez, "Intelligence Agents or Students?"

114. Cited in ibid.

115. Ketcham, "The Israeli Art Student Mystery."

116. Cited in ibid.

117. Ibid.

118. Cited in ibid.

119. Ibid.

120. Nathan Guttman, "Spies, or Students?", *Ha'aretz*, May 13, 2002; http://216.239.33.100/search?q=cache:a4CifBJsiLIC: www.commondreams.org/headlines02/ 0513-05.htm+%22israeli+art+students%22+salon+&hl=en&ie=UTF-8.

121. See Metafilter.com, May 28, 2002; http://www.metafilter.com/mefi/ 17005.

122. "Tapped," *The American Prospect*, May 8, 2002; http://www. prospect.org/webfeatures/2002/05/tapped-s-05-06.html#745amart.

123. Robert Rudolph, Kate Coscarreli, and Brian Donohue, "Evidence takes investigators through Wayne and Fort Lee," *Newark* [New Jersey] *Star-Ledger*, September 15, 2001.

124. "NJ Locations Searched In Connection With Terror Attacks; Airport Shut Down Again," WABC-TV, New York, September 14, 2001; http://abclocal.go.com/wabc/news/WABC_091401_airports.html.

125. Adam Lisberg, "Five hijack suspects had links to N.J.,"Bergen County [New Jersey] *Record*, September 15, 2001.

126. Press release, "State Granted Access to Moving Company's Storage Facility," New Jersey Department of Law and Public Safety (Division of Consumer Affairs), December 13, 2001; http://www.state.nj.us/lps/ca/press/ storage.htm.

127. Marc Perelman, "Spy Rumours Fly on Gusts of Truth," *Forward*, March 15, 2002.

128. Stewart Ain, "Caught in a Dragnet," *The Jewish Week*, December 2, 2001.

129. Chris Isham, John Miller, Glenn Silber and Chris Vlasto, "The White Van: Were Israelis Detained on Sept. 11 Spies?", ABC News, June 21, 2002; http://abcnews.go.com/sections/2020/DailyNews/ 2020_whitevan_020621.html.

130. Ain, "Caught in a Dragnet."

131. James Risen and Don Van Natta, Jr., "Authorities Have Learned the Identities of 18 Hijackers, Attorney General Says," *New York Times*, September 14, 2001; http://www.crimelynx.com/identhij.html.

132. "The White Van," ABC News, June 21, 2002.

133. Paulo Lima, "Five Men Detained As Suspected Conspirators," *Bergen County Record*, September 12, 2001; A8.

134. http://cryptome.org/Finnlist.pdf;   http://cryptome.orig/CI-08-02.pdf. Also: www.antiwar.com/justin/CI-08-02.pdf.

135. web.tiscali.it/factandnews/Files/CIRCOLARI%202002/CI-03-02.pdf

136. Lima, "Five Men Detained…"

137. The release of this material has provoked attempts to debunk the accuracy of the various lists in circulation. The *Wall Street Journal* led the parade with a story headlined "FBI's post-9/11 watch list spreads far, mutates."[November 19, 2002] The story relates a number of deficiencies in what the FBI called "Operation Lookout": faxed copies of the suspect lists that were later transcribed inaccurately, mixing up persons with identical or similar names, and a basic misapprehension of the purpose of the watch lists, which is described as consisting merely of persons the authorities "want to talk to." Distribution of the lists was stopped after six weeks, and soon became "obsolete," the writer assures us. Furthermore, we are told by a news report on CNN, the list "contains names of people who have been cleared of any possible connection to last year's attacks." The claim is that the suspect lists were entirely the product of "the crisis atmosphere right after the terror attacks"—before the U.S. government tightened security and started covering up any trails that might lead to the Israeli connection. "A year later," we are told, "the list has taken on a life of its own, multiplying—and error-filled—versions being passed around like bootleg music." [Kelli Arena, "U.S. watch list has 'taken on life of its own,' FBI says," CNN, November 20, 2002.]

However, the list cited here contains not only the names of individuals, some with American names and addresses, but also a number of businesses. One entry I found particularly intriguing was the Crown Fried Chicken Corporation of 131 Morgan Avenue, in Brooklyn, New York. The list was posted in May 2002. In September, U.S. prosecutors announced that the company was a front for Al-Qaeda-connected drug operations. FBI officials "have characterized the investigation as 'one of the most important being run out of our New York office,'" reported the *New York Sun* [September 23, 2002]. FBI officials now say they have "lost control" of the lists. But what they have lost control of is a key piece of evidence linking an Israeli spy nest to the horrific events of 9/11—and they are scrambling to rein it in.

138. Oliver Schröm, "Next Door to Mohamed Atta," *Die Zeit*, October 14, 2002: http://iraq-info.1accesshost.com/schrom.html.

139. Ibid.

140. Ibid.

141. Ibid.

142. Ibid.

143. John Sugg, "The spies who came in from the art sale," *Weekly Planet*, March 20, 2002; http://atlanta.creativeloafing.com/2002-03-20/fishwrapper.html

144. Matthias Gebauer,"Mossad Agents Were On Atta's Heals," *Der Spiegel*, October 1, 2002; http://www.spiegel.de/politik/ausland/0,1518,216421,00.html.

145. Ibid.

146. Ibid.

147. December 11, 2001; http://www.firefox.1accesshost.com/cameron.html.

148. "The White Van," http://abcnews.go.com/sections/2020/DailyNews/2020_whitevan_020621.html.

149. Ibid.

150. David Hirst, *The Gun and the Olive Branch*, 1977, 1984, Futura Publications.

151. Doron Geller,"The Lavon Affair," The Pedagogic Center, Department for Jewish Zionist Education, Jewish Agency for Israel, 1997, http://www.jajz-ed.org.il/juice/service/week2.html.

152. Ibid.

153. Ibid.

154. Hirst, *The Gun and the Olive Branch*.

155. Ibid.

156. *New York Times*, February 10, 1961.

157. Ibid.

158. Eric Margolis, "Mideast Murder, Inc.," *Toronto Sun*, October 14, 1997.

159. Seymour M. Hersh, "The Case Against Jonathan Pollard," *The New Yorker*, January 18, 1999, pp. 26-33.

160. Hirst, *The Gun and the Olive Branch*.

161. Diala Saadeh, "Palestinians: Israel Faked Gaza Al Qaeda Presence," Reuters via ABC News, December 7, 2002; http://abcnews.go.com/wire/World/reuters20021207_65.html.

162. See also Sophie Claudet, "Palestinian Authority uncovers Israelis posing as Al-Qaeda agents," *Middle East Online*, December 7, 2002; http://www.middle-east-online.com/english/?id=3544.

163. Saadeh, "Israel Faked…"

164. See also Danny Rubinstein, "Ibrahim, the Shin Bet wants you to join Qaida," *Ha'aretz*, December 18, 2002; http://www.haaretzdaily.com/hasen/pages/ShArt.jhtml?itemNo=241042.

165. John Mintz, "Al Qaeda targets Israelis: website," *Washington Post*, December 7 2002; http://www.theage.com.au/handheld/articles/2002/12/06/1038950195289.htm.

166. Paul W. Schroeder, "The Case Against Preemptive War," *The American Conservative*, October 21, 2002.

167. Andrew Sullivan, "Anti-semitism sneaks into the antiwar camp," *Times* of London, October 20, 2002.

168. James V. Grimaldi, "2 FBI Whistle-Blowers Allege Lax Security, Possible Espionage," *Washington Post*, June 19, 2002.

169. James V. Grimaldi, "Senators Criticize FBI, Justice Whistle-Blower's Allegations Ignored, Lawmakers Say," *Washington Post*, August 14, 2002.

170. Stephen J. Hedges, "Senators ask attorney general to review former FBI linguist's claims against colleague," *Chicago Tribune*, August 13 2002.

171. "Did FBI Deliberately Slow Translation?," *Sixty Minutes*, CBS News, October 25, 2002; http://www.cbsnews.com/stories/2002/10/25/60minutes/main526954.shtml.

172. Eric Margolis, "Turkey: Where East reluctantly meets West," *Toronto Sun*, June 6, 2002; http://www.bigeye.com/060602.htm.

173. Gordon Thomas, "Mossad Spymaster Efraim Halevy," Gordonthomas.ie, September 2001; http://www.gordonthomas.ie/Articles/spymaster.htm.

174. Grimaldi, "2 FBI Whistle-Blowers Allege Lax Security."

175. Ibid.

176. Senators Charles L. Grassley and Patrick Leahy, Letter to Attorney General John Ashcroft, August 13, 2002; http://leahy.senate.gov/press/200208/081302.html.

177. Walter Pincus and Dana Priest, "NSA Intercepts On Eve of 9/11 Sent a Warning," *Washington Post*, June 20, 2002; http://www.washingtonpost.com/ac2/wp-dyn?pagename=article&node=&contentId=A12712-2002Jun19&notFound=true.

178. "Statement of the Attorneys for FBI Whistleblower Sibel Edmonds," Washington, D.C., June 19, 2002; http://www.whistleblowers.org/edmunds.htm.

179. "Statement of Barbara Comstock, Director of Public Affairs, Regarding Today's Filing in Sibel Edmonds v. Department of Justice," Department of Justice, October 18, 2002; http://www.usdoj.gov/opa/pr/2002/October/02_ag_605.htm.

180. Michael Isikoff And Evan Thomas, "The Saudi Money Trail," *Newsweek*, December 2, 2002; http://stacks.msnbc.com/news/839269.asp.

181. Sami Peretz, "Accounts in Israeli banks used for terrorism, central bank believes," *Ha'aretz*, November 31, 2002; http://www.haaretzdaily.com/hasen/pages/ShArt.jhtml?itemNo=206537&contrassID=2&subContrassID=2&sbSubContrassID=0&listSrc=Y&itemNo=206537.

182. Ibid.

183. "Improving Intelligence," PBS *News Hour*, December 11, 2002; http://www.pbs.org/newshour/bb/congress/july-dec02/intelligence_12-11.html.

184. Ibid.

185. Ibid.

186. Christopher Ketcham, "The Israeli Art Student Mystery."

0-595-29682-3